WHO'S
WHO *of*
DOGS

WHO'S
WHO *of*
DOGS

JOHN R. F. BREEN
EDITOR

WORKMAN PUBLISHING, NEW YORK

The material originally appeared in *Who's Who of Animals
1992* and *Who's Who of Animals 1993*.

Library of Congress Cataloguing-in-Publication Data

Who's who of dogs / by John R. F. Breen, editor.
p.   cm.
ISBN 1-56305-871-5 (pbk.)
1. Dogs—United States—Biography.   I. Breen, John R. F.
SF426.2.W49   1995
636.7'00973—dc20   94-44826
                                                        CIP

Workman books are available at special discounts when purchased in bulk for premiums and sales promotions as well as
for fund-raising or educational use. Special editions or book
excerpts can also be created to specification. For details,
please contact the Special Sales Director at the address below.

Workman Publishing
708 Broadway
New York, NY 10003-9555
Manufactured in the United States of America
10   9   8   7   6   5   4   3   2   1

INTRODUCTION

What do you think of when you hear the word *dog*? Although there are many breeds of dogs, chances are it's a big, lovable mutt who leaps into your mind. And it's not only the dog who bowls you over; it's also the dog's personality. This is the kind of dog you will find honored again and again in this *Who's Who of Dogs*.

Imagine a world without such friendly, good-natured dogs. Think how ornery people would be. Every day millions of dog owners walk their dogs, run into other dog owners, and exchange pleasantries (as do the dogs). There is a dignified, ritualized, and *civilized* greeting given by all. Now consider if they were all walking their cats instead—everyone would be snarling and clawing and hissing at each other.

Moreover, all these dog owners come home each day and pat their dogs who, inevitably, are ecstatic. Think what this does for the owners' flagging spirits. Here they are, home after being subjected to the usual indignities and humiliations, and someone actually wants to see them. So, in addition to making civilization possible, dogs have the good sense to make it a happy one.

Now, in theory, a human *Who's Who* lists people who have achieved something noteworthy in their lives—people who *are* somebody. Such people are also, of course, generally insufferable. Not so with the dogs in this *Who's Who*! These canines not only are special, but they're creatures you'd be glad to have as friends. Who wouldn't want to invite any of these dogs over for dinner? They just sparkle with humor and personality.

In fact, when you think about it, it's a good thing that a human *Who's Who* excludes dogs. Otherwise there would be no room for the humans. Try to think of even one person who is as honorable, generous, kind, steadfast, altruistic, and above all gung-ho as your average dog. Dogs possess every trait that humans aspire to for a few hours at best before it all gets too much for them and they revert to their normal selves.

The biographies of the dogs contained herein originally appeared in *Who's Who of Animals*. They were written by the human friends and colleagues of the dogs, people who had the honor to be in the presence of such magnificent canines for extended periods of time. As you read these biographies, you will see that we are, indeed, privileged to be dog's best friend.

John R. F. Breen

AAGELYNN'S LADY KATE
LOSQUADRO
NEW YORK, NEW YORK

K atie took a flying leap into life on February 5, 1986, and immediately let it be known that she was boss. The first to climb out of the birthing box and the most ferocious, she is the leader of the pack. At two, she gave birth to Pete and Nicki and surprised all with her mothering skills. Though very aggressive, this seven-pound Maltese is a real mush and only demands treats and neck scratching. The second member of "The Terrors of 14th Street," she has but one love—her brother Spencer, of course!

ABBEY OF GLENBROOK RD.
STAMFORD, CONNECTICUT

Abbey has been trained to say his prayers; he bows his head and waits motionless until the "Our Father" prayer has been completed, then raises his head. He has three stuffed animals that he plays with and takes to his bed, which is called his Condo. He knows the animals by name and will pick them up when told to. He picks his leash up when he is told we are going for a walk. He knows how to sit-wait (he licks his chops before he eats), also to drop dead.

Abbey McDaniel
Granite City, Illinois

Abbey is a five-and-a-half-year-old Beagle who still acts like a puppy. She loves to be hugged and to sleep on your lap. She also loves children and friendly hands. Abbey's only hatred is of cats—she can "hear" them walk down the street. She was adopted from the Humane Society in 1988 after being found running rabbits "on the streets." She now rules our home as the queen and barks her orders to all of us. Her only vice is to burrow under the covers of the bed after we've left for work. Abbey was our first and is deeply loved.

ABERYSWYTH CYMRU AM BETH
MIDWAY CITY, CALIFORNIA

A beryswyth, or Abby, is a six-month-old sable Welsh Cardigan Corgi. She is an active, sweet-tempered pup who busily makes the world her playground. This little Pippit loves to jump in her pool and then race around the yard looking for someone to share her wetness with. She worships the older dogs and learns from each one, though not always things her humans want her to copy. As a natural alarm clock, she joyfully awakens each of us with bounces and kisses. And we all rest when she takes a nap.

ABIDING FAITH BERKMAN
NEW YORK, NEW YORK

Abiding Faith is a nine-year-old, black-and-tan Terrier/Doberman/Spaniel/Gordon Setter mix (it all depends on the angle). From head on, she looks like a fox with airplane-wing ears. When she first arrived at the age of seven months, she decided that her job was to fight every dog in sight, so she was taken to "military school," where she soon turned into a star pupil. Her best trick is levitating straight up into my arms from a sitting position at my feet.

ACAR CANI ("THUG") MECHTA
DELANO, TENNESSEE

Every last ounce of Thug's 115 pounds breathes pure Anatolian Shepherd. He came to the farm as a pup to guard the flock and discourage feral ruffians, and he does quite a fine job. His authoritative presence has been rather intimidating. Yet he loves the sheep, licking their noses when they permit and contentedly observing them when they don't. On the few occasions when he is taken on an adventure away from home, Thug is found basking in the attentions of his human admirers, never getting enough. Such demure eyes he offers to the good at heart!

ALBERT EINSTEIN LANAHAN
CHICAGO, ILLINOIS

Albert is a four-year-old, tricolor male Basset Hound, son of Broadway Joe and Dolly Parton, and favorite grandson of Jane. Albert is a media mogul and famous model. When Burberry of London needed a model, Albert was their Hush Puppy. Albert has appeared twice on network television, and he has appeared in feature news and fashion articles in syndicated newspapers. He was Mayor Richard M. Daley's accompanist in the 1993 Southside Irish Parade in Chicago. Albert is available for modeling assignments. His earnings go to charity.

7

ALEX ("BIG AL") LENGEL
MOSCOW, PENNSYLVANIA

Big, bad, and beautiful, this lovable and loyal black Lab has a "lapdog" mentality. When not swimming, he can be seen hurling a two-by-four through the air and catching it; galloping through the streets with a tree limb balanced between his teeth; or playing "running back" with his jaws locked around a pigskin to test his agility against humans. Otherwise, he merely relaxes on a grassy knoll. His favorite pastime is cruisin' around in a black BMW with Greg, the Lengel son. He eats everything from decorative bark to Bokhara rugs, and loves his daily romps through the woods with his master, Jack, "marking" everything.

ALEXIA GREEN MOUNTAIN GIRL
FARMINGTON, CONNECTICUT

Lexi, a 21-month-old female Labrador Retriever, loves people and food. She is being trained for assistance work and so far is able to pick up the telephone, ring a doorbell, turn on lights, and call an elevator. For pleasure, Lexi likes to play ball, retrieve almost anything, and swim in any water she can find. When she is not working, Lexi spends most of the day chasing and wrestling with her Siberian Husky housemate.

ALFIE MIZUFUKA A.K.C. "LITTLE PRINCETON"
HAWTHORNE, CALIFORNIA

In loving memory of Alfie. (March 1968–May 1982). Alfie was my very first Yorkshire Terrier. His Father was "Seldom Seen Same," his Mother "Piskey of Mohave." He weighed eight pounds and had silver and tan markings. Unlike most Yorkies, Alfie's left ear drooped and the right one stood up! Alfie was a loving and loyal companion to our family, always ready to protect and defend. He eagerly learned new tricks and patiently awaited the rewards that followed them. He loved walks, car rides, squeaky toys, and balloons! But most of all, he left a legacy of very fond memories.

ALICE ("THE LITTLE RIVER FREIGHT TRAIN") BAGLEY
FT. LAUDERDALE, FLORIDA

Alice is a twelve-year-old American Pit Bull Terrier. She's never been clipped or cropped and is very fat, so she looks like a fat old red pig. She loves to eat what humans eat, sleep where humans sleep, and go for rides in the car. Alice's sweet, gentle disposition and happy face make friends out of disbelievers, even the mailman. Most of all, she's a good, loyal pal. Like I've always said, "I'd rather be around my dog Alice than most people I know."

AMANDA KEMPLER
WEST ORANGE, NEW JERSEY

Mandy is a very sweet fourteen-year-old white-and-liver English Springer Spaniel who is a semiretired mascot of St. Hubert's Giralda Animal Welfare and Education Center in Madison, New Jersey. Her wonderful career consists of being petted by schoolchildren and nursing home residents. When Mandy is not working, she spends her days with us either sleeping, eating or vacuuming the house of all food particles. Even though Mandy doesn't hear or see well anymore, she still enjoys vacationing in Cape Cod, where she can run in the water, chase the birds, and just be a Springer.

AMAZING GRACE BERKMAN
NEW YORK, NEW YORK

Amazing Grace is a twelve-year-old black Spaniel/Labrador Retriever mix who is more amazing than graceful. Her most amazing outdoor stunt involves pressing the side of her face to the ground, raising her rump, and wagging her tail full swing, all the while looking out of the corner of her eye at the crowds that gather around. The children in the neighborhood call her "The Dog Who Tries to Stand on Her Head." Pretty good for a dog who started life abandoned on the mean streets of New York.

AMBER ("AMBERCROMBIE") SIPKA
AKRON, OHIO

An eighty-five-pound gorgeous wheat-colored purebred yellow Lab female and a pure kissy-face bundle of love. At age three, she loves to catch her ball and keep her seven-year-old black Lab stepbrother as young as she is. She smiles constantly and loves to wrestle. Favorite treats: strawberries, melons, apples, carrots, and pizza. She's a perfect nurse as she crawls next to you to keep you warm and kisses your face to make you well. She's always ready to play ball and more than balances the sometimes ugly world with her love and affection. She's God's gift!

CAN. CH., U-UD AMBERAC'S GAETY AT HONEYCOMB
AM.BER.CAN.UD, S-CDX, JH, AM.CAN.WD, TT, CGC, TDI, VC
LAKEWOOD, NEW JERSEY

Gae has 22 titles in three countries and is one of the most titled Golden Retrievers in the history of the breed in this country. For many years, she visited the elderly in several nursing homes where her smiling face brought joy to all. At age 13 plus, her body has slowed, her steps are not as agile as they once were, but her spirit is alive and well and the smile is still there. Gae is my best friend and it has been my privilege to share her life.

AMIGO NYSTROM
AURORA, COLORADO

A migo is a small tan-and-white female Chihuahua. She enjoys hibernating during the cold winter months and fishing during the warm summer months. The Cache La Poudre River is her favorite fishing hole. It is along this river that Amigo and her best friend, Jeff, seek refuge from life in the big city. Although Jeff catches all the fish, Amigo is always at his side to make sure the "big one" doesn't get away. After a hard day of fishing, Amigo can be found roaming the woods in search of small animals or lying in the tall grass eating insects.

ANGELA ("HONEY-HOCKS") GOOD-DOG
TUCSON, ARIZONA

From a shy, apologetic puppy who appeared from next door, Angie matured into an enlightened little Buddha in a dog suit. Her sweet nature, simple wisdom, and eagerness to please were gifts that taught me much about creating harmony. In return, I felt privileged to be her lifetime companion and guardian. We shared my meals, modeled for art class together, and ventured into the wilderness like two intrepid explorers. She favored fast rides in the cab of my Chevy pickup. I treasure most my memories of quiet, meditative morning dog walks through intriguing back alleys. Our love endures.

ANGEL-ALDINE
PLAINFIELD, CONNECTICUT

Angel-Aldine is a retired racing Greyhound. She's extremely friendly and enjoys being around people, especially children. One of her favorite pastimes is dressing in different costumes during various holidays and special occasions. Since she retired, her participation has won her three blue ribbons. The ribbons include: Kiwanis International, Lower Camden County Dog Training Club for Best Costume and First Place for the Pointiest Nose at the Seventh Annual Animal Celebration (Cathedral of St. John the Divine). Her favorite pastime is attending polo games at Hidden Pond, Winslow Township, New Jersey. Although her tiger-like appearance fools a lot of people, inside is the warm gentleness of a lamb.

ANNABELLE BREEN
DEDHAM, MASSACHUSETTS

Annabelle is a twelve-year-old blond Shih Tzu/Dachshund. Her tail is almost as big as herself; when she wags it (all the time), it goes around in a circle like an airplane propeller. Annabelle resembles a stuffed teddy bear. Several years ago she went into a deep depression when her black-and-white Setter friend Nando died. The wonderful tail never wagged, and she looked very sad. Only after a year with our new Sheltie puppy Laddie did she return to her old self. Annabelle is everyone's favorite dog, and children and adults gravitate to her instinctively.

ANNETTE'S BAD BOY TERMINATOR
MESQUITE, TEXAS

Terminator is a spunky one-year-old male Doberman Pinscher. Officially registered as Annette's Bad Boy Terminator, he prefers just to be called Terminator. Whether he's chewing on the doghouse, carrying his food bowl around the yard, or blowing bubbles in the water bucket, Terminator is a happy dog who provides plenty of entertainment! Although he sometimes lives up to his name, Bad Boy, he is sure to grow up and be a well-behaved gentleman. But now he's a young pup with a lifetime of dreams.

ANNIE ADAMS
VERO BEACH, FLORIDA

Annie is a blond Cocker Spaniel who loves to eat! Her favorites are pizza crusts and chicken. Annie refuses to drink tap water out of a regular dog bowl, however, because her ears get wet, so she drinks ice-cold water out of a juice glass. Her favorite toys are bones, stuffed animals, balls, and socks. Annie loves to play tug-of-war with any type of socks. She also loves hunting lizards, but most of the time they're too fast for her. When she does catch one, she's so surprised she accidentally lets go of it!

ANNIE BAGPIPES MACDOUGALL JOHNSON
SALEM, MASSACHUSETTS

Part Springer Spaniel, part Wirehair Fox Terrier, Annie was an incredibly sweet dog. She looked like a Victorian circus dog. She had scruffy white fur with a black mask. Annie shed hair for a living and was very good at it. She could climb trees and ate alpine strawberries from the garden. If you sang the song "Oklahoma," she'd lick your face in a frenzy. Annie loved to run in the local cemetery and would run fast and low to the ground. She hated mushrooms and would spit them out if they were in her food.

ANTHONY JON BARNUM
GAINESVILLE, FLORIDA

Tony is a six-and-a-half-year-old Lhasa Apso. When I first saw him in the pet store, I knew he was coming home with me, and we have been together ever since. Tony is like my own flesh and blood and is very pampered. He never lets me out of his sight. His favorite food is tomatoes. His favorite place is my bedroom windowsill, which is also where he sleeps when he isn't sleeping on my pillow. When it's hot outside, he loves sitting on the top steps of the pool. I love Tony with all my heart.

ARCHIBALD COLALILLO
KENILWORTH, NEW JERSEY

I remember the day my parents and I went to pick up Archie, now 15 years old. We had seen an ad in the local newspaper in which a family was selling the puppies from their dog's litter. Archibald was one of those puppies. He is a beautiful mix (half Keeshond, half Norwegian Elkhound). Over the years Arch, with his white paws and tan legs, has brought our family much happiness and many memories. None of us will forget his healthy appetite for soap, chocolate cake, gum, and pasta. He will remain a legend in our house.

ARIEL ("ARIELLA BOBELLA") CROUCH
CELINA, OHIO

Ariel is a feisty, petite black-and-white Rat Terrier. She is a warm-weather girl who loves the summer sun. During the cold winter months she likes to take her daily jog around the tables and chairs in her living room. Even though Ariel is the smallest of her two siblings, she prefers to think that she is the one with the most authority and she tries to show it whenever she can. While relaxing at night, her favorite place is under her dad's shirt, nice and warm. Ariel's favorite foods include chicken and cauliflower.

ARIEL ("SCARIEL")
AKRON, OHIO

Ariel is a mixed-breed dog who is full of fun and feist! She has mahogany toenails and weighs all of twenty pounds, but she patrols the backyard as if she's ten times bigger! She has been instrumental in introducing my niece to the dog world. She *loves* sitting in front of my furnace register when it's chilly. She's the first to welcome anyone in my house and the first to warn of anything or anyone on the property. She likes to car-ride and go to any park. She carries a toy or ball in her mouth all day, every day, most of which are bigger than she is!

ASHBY
WORCESTER, MASSACHUSETTS

Ashby is a fourteen-year-old Peke-A-Poo who has become somewhat of a legend in his hometown. For most of his life, he has been taking a taxicab by himself to and from the groomers. His owner, a designer and journalist, simply calls a cab, puts his tip under the collar, and opens the front door. When the groomer is finished, Ashby makes the return trip home. He has earned the equivalent of about five college degrees and has written for the "On The Road" column of *Worcester Magazine*. Ashby is assisted in his adventures by a three-year-old English tabby named Lily.

Ashleen Flaherty
New York, New York

Ashleen Flaherty is an eight-month-old Blenheim Cavalier King Charles Spaniel. Her name means "A Beautiful Dream" in Gaelic. And she is exactly that, with deep brown eyes, a sweet face, and the most adorable way of demanding affection. I had mixed feelings about getting a second "fur person" because of my deep love for Liam. But I find I have plenty of love to give them both. Our life wouldn't be as joyful without the Girls.

A TOUCH OF SUNSHINE
WINSTON-SALEM, NORTH CAROLINA

A Touch of Sunshine, and that she is, is a two-year-old yellow Labrador Retriever, special in every way. Sunshine has had torn ligaments in both her knees, which required two surgeries and many months of recuperation. During that time she ate shoes, a bathroom wall, a wallet, a couple of bed pillows, two sets of bed sheets, several comforters, a bed skirt, and a bedroom wall. Sunshine's favorite hobby is to go to the beach and ride the waves. She's a true companion; she even goes to work with me in a business office. Sunshine, that she is.

AXEL VON ROMMEL HABERCHAK
APOLLO, PENNSYLVANIA

Whelped June 20, 1991, Axel is an AKC-registered Rottweiler who thinks he is a human child. True to his herding instinct, he uses his body to guide his humans where he wants them. His favorite toys are frisbees, balls, Grandpa's galoshes, and sometimes clean laundry that he will steal out of the dryer. He never lets his dad out of his sight for long. In fact, he will lie on his dad's feet just to make sure he doesn't wander down to the creek without him.

BABAR BRINKMAN
INDIANAPOLIS, INDIANA

Babar, an Old English Sheepdog, is three years old, black with four white feet. He loves to talk to people with his squeaky toys and hops around everywhere when playing tug-of-war. At over 100 pounds of fluffy fur, he can clear quite a path! He also is very ready to curl up and take a nap with you anytime you say so, but his favorite treat is the large bowl of ice he gets nightly. He waits in the same place every night and crunches away until he goes to bed with a cool belly full of ice and a warm pillow under his head.

BABY
PITTSBURGH, PENNSYLVANIA

My best friend, Baby, is a dog who is part German Shepherd and part Collie. She's tall, blond, and has a beautiful black face. Baby is playful and has a great sense of humor. She loves to run in wide open fields, steal socks, bury her bones underneath the pillows on my bed, and sit on people's heads when they're lying down! Baby is a great companion, and I love her very much.

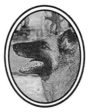

BABY "BABAS" HOWELL
PITTSBURGH, PENNSYLVANIA

Baby came into my life as a puppy on April 10, 1989, and we've been best friends ever since. Baby has a personality all her own and loves such things as searching my shopping bags for the treats she knows that I always buy for her, chasing squirrels, playing in a nearby pond, and having the insides of her ears scratched. She loathes the vacuum, thunderstorms, and being sprayed with perfume.

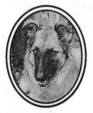

BAILEY CASTILLO
LAS VEGAS, NEVADA

Bailey is a human disguised as a Cocker Spaniel. He loves to play with balls and has about seven of them that he keeps around him at all times. If his parents try to pick up the balls and put them in his toy basket, he becomes very upset and will take them out one by one until they are all over the floor again! He loves to push the balls with his tongue; he'll roll them underneath the furniture and then cry when he can't reach them. His favorite song is "Kumbaya," sung by his dad.

BAM'S SWEET SPENCER G'BOY MANCUSO
NEW YORK, NEW YORK

A six-pound Maltese born February 5, 1986, the last of three pups, Spencer arrived feet first, purple and not breathing. He was hand-rubbed to life and returned to his mother and two sisters within half an hour. A bundle of love and a bit of a rogue, Spencer has one passion, his sister Kate, with whom he lives. A real gentledog, he always puts the ladydogs first and once went nose to nose with two Dobermans to protect his mom and sister. As a team Spencer and Kate are "The Terrors of 14th Street," ganging up on all the neighborhood dogs and winning, of course!

BANDIT
LYNN, INDIANA

A Collie/Shepherd mix who loves children and hates thieves, Bandit guards every house in sight. She likes to play with other animals, especially a two-year-old Schipperke of ours. The police have a very high opinion of Bandit—she stopped a burglary in our neighbor's garage by breaking out of my barn and taking the stolen goods away from them. Since that night there have been no robberies in our neighborhood.

BANDIT ("THE B") MALOTT

B orn December 20, 1985, in a canine nursery from hell, Bandit, our 100-pound Malamute mix, has "come a long way, doggie." From abandonment and abuse, Bandit now ranks with dogdom's elite. He has a heated, air-conditioned, couch-laden room for "time-outs" when his big-footed antics overwhelm guests or the cat. Three times a day, Bandit challenges my husband to an around-the-block tug-of-war. His talents include "slurplessly" mouthing tissues, wallets, or glasses out of pockets and singing on key with perfect howl modulation. Thank you, "B," for being the best of man's best friends.

BARNEY AND BABE PRISBREY
WEBSTER GROVES, MISSOURI

We have two dogs: one Cocker named Barney and one abandoned Lhasa mix named Babe. They are best friends. When Barney was in the hospital recently, Babe was listless and so depressed that she wouldn't eat. Barney had surgery for a dental problem. When he came out of the anesthetic, my husband took Babe to visit Barney in the hospital. Babe's tail wagged with happiness. My husband asked the vet if Babe could spend the night in the hospital with Barney. The vet agreed. Barney and Babe came home the following day. Two happy animals.

BARNEY LYNCH
EAST FALMOUTH, MASSACHUSETTS

Barney was born November 11, 1982, a beautiful English Golden Retriever. He's been going to the beach since he was a pup. His favorite pastime is taking a boat ride over to Washburn's Island and spending the day diving for rocks! I've had many dogs in my time, but none compare to good ole' "Barn." He is the most loving, loyal companion. Of course, the fact that I spoil him rotten and feed him bacon and eggs, and pizza, has caused people to call him the Cholesterol Canine! It's no wonder he's so devoted to me! He is my best friend. I love him dearly.

BARNEY ("THE BEAGLE") WILLIAMS
NEWARK, DELAWARE

Mike and Susan Williams bought little Barney in a local convenience store for the staggering sum of $40. A purebred Beagle with no papers, he's a whole lot of puppy. He has developed into a proud example of his breed: full of fun, mischievous, active, ornery, tough as nails, overflowing with love, and on occasion—obedient. Barney doesn't bark, he yowls, and when he does, the house shakes and he recoils at least two feet backward. He has now entered puppy obedience training and is showing great promise. Barney "The Beagle" is now a respected member of the Williams household.

BARON HAENSSLER
SELIGENSTADT, GERMANY

Baron is a seven-year-old Weimaraner who was born a hunting dog. One summer day Baron came into our living room from the garden with a strange expression on his face. Suddenly there was the whistle of a bird in the room. But there was no bird. And again a whistle. Baron's mouth was closed—which was unusual for a dog. I pried his mouth open and a bird jumped out. But Baron jumped also and the bird was again "jailed" in his mouth. Finally we managed to free the bird, unharmed, although Baron was naturally disappointed. He's a nice dog who likes to hunt!

BARTHOLOMEW OF FERNCLIFF
CHARLOTTE, NORTH CAROLINA

Barthley is an extroverted English Springer Spaniel. Born in August 1986, she is a true Leo. She loves visitors and constantly interrupts conversations to keep the focus on herself. More than anything, she hates to be "in the doghouse" and assumes a sad, soulful expression until she's back in good graces. She keeps an eagle eye on shoes and sunglasses, which signal an outing; if not included, she mournfully retreats to her chair. Favorite activities are catching the ball and riding in the car. She loves the water and puts on quite a show when diving in concert with her mistress.

BASHART HLAVATY
CHICAGO, ILLINOIS

Bashart (Buh-Shairt) was left/lost in the park. When no owner could be found, he became part of the family. His new sister, Cocoa, is just thrilled to have a playmate that is her size. Bashart is a friendly, mostly obedient dog who quickly became very protective of his new home. He likes to play with his new siblings but needs to be more gentle with the cats. He is very athletic, and I quickly discovered he can jump all my fences. Luckily I have money available for taller ones. Time for training!

BEAR BAKER
PAGOSA SPRINGS, COLORADO

Bear is a "bigger than life" dog with a spirit to match. He is an Australian Shepherd/ Lab mix. Bear can do anything required of him, from helping bring in firewood to loading a truck with tree branches. He works for his dad, Jerry, and always provides companionship and moral support for his whole family. He will always remain in our hearts, and we feel we are better people for knowing him.

Bear McDaniel
Granite City, Illinois

Bear is a three-and-a-half-year-old black dog with light brown markings (he may be a Labrador and Rottweiler mix). He is extremely protective of his mistress, who found him on a country road when he was only 1.4 pounds and nursed him back to life. He loves to go for car rides and sits up, on the passenger side, leaning against the door. Bear knows he is the king of the house, but he can act modest. He loves women but is not so fond of children, men, or uniforms. Bear is our second and yet our baby boy—he is loved.

BEAR GAIT'S "NAPALOTT"
SHERMAN OAKS, CALIFORNIA

Napalott is our Int'l Champion Neapolitan Mastiff. He is two and a half years old and weighs 120 pounds (but he thinks he weighs 10 pounds and leans against you, almost knocking you over). He believes he's human. It's fun to watch him try to vocally interject his opinion during your conversation. He loves playing tug-of-war, snoring louder than anyone in the house, and getting on the bed and wiping his drool on you. Nappy is our big baby, who wouldn't hurt a fly and wants to play all day long.

BEATLEBUG
BRANDON, FLORIDA

Brown almond eyes, watching every move I make. Black curls and waves of fur, wild if not cut. She's a hundred percent purebred mutt! Resting her head on the windowsill to watch all that goes on outside. Her best fuzzy friend is a fourteen-year-old cat, Kasper. Together they soak up the sunshine. She didn't choose to be born or dumped on the street, but has chosen me as her companion. I will forever love her and take care of her, that happy shaggy dog with the constant smile, Gubby.

BEAU DAVIS
CORNELIA, GEORGIA

Beau is a red-gold Golden Retriever and my best friend. He picked me out at a time when I was very sad, having just lost my father. He has been my protector and friend, and can always make me laugh. His favorite hobby is collecting tennis balls. When he was young (he's six now), he ate all my pierced earrings and had to have two operations on his stomach. He loves running in the woods and chasing deer, rabbits, and possums, etc. I hope I can give him a wonderful life, because he has given me the greatest gift of all—his devotion and love.

BEAUREGARD DE CHANTILLY
JONQUIERE, QUEBEC, CANADA

Beauregard is pure Bloodhound. He takes after his grandmother on his father's side, a dashing dog indeed. At twelve weeks he left Missouri (not his idea) and landed in a pile of snow—Quebec. However, since he learned French, it's not so bad. Now he spends his days herding cats and writing letters (to Missouri Molly, his Mommy), though he gets more ink on the rugs than on the paper. This makes his mistress get red in the face and yell. Then she takes him for a walk, all the while mumbling something about "a one-way ticket back to Goodman." Beauregard wonders: Is Goodman in Missouri?

BEBE HANSON DOUGLAS
VISTA, CALIFORNIA

BeBe is a thirteen-year-old white Lhasa Apso/Poodle mix. Everyone thinks she is still a puppy because she has such a playful spirit. BeBe has brought great happiness to her family. She has such human qualities that we forget she is a dog—she's just one of the kids. BeBe loves to play with her favorite toy, a black-and-red furry ball. She loves to catch rays of sun coming in the window for an occasional sunbath. Her favorite treats are bell peppers and avocado and she loves Pupperoni dog treats. But most of all she loves us and we love her!

BELLE ("BELLY BOO") PAUL
LAKEWOOD, COLORADO

Belle is an eight-year-old, spayed black-and-red Bouvier des Flandres/Irish Setter. She loves to run and play ball, and personally selects toys from either her indoor or outdoor toy box. I have never seen her tired. She is a well-mannered lady but is suspicious of strangers, especially metermen. She has long, wavy hair and looks like she has antennae when her hair sticks up. She has expressive eyes and looks either ecstatic or depressed, never in between. She went Christmas caroling at a nursing home with me once. She thinks our guinea pigs are puppies.

51

BENTLEY ("B") KING
DURHAM, NORTH CAROLINA

Bentley is a seven-year-old, 140-pound English Mastiff who is extremely friendly. He loves to try to chase rabbits and squirrels. Bentley is the Housemaster. He sleeps anywhere, and while napping will sleep on his back, feet up in the air. (What a sight!) His favorite activity is taking rides with the wind blowing in his face—jaws blown out and opened. Bentley has his own room with fan, sleeping sofa, night-light, and TV (stays on CNN). He only gives love and is a pleasure for his owner. Bentley was adopted from a wonderful lady who sees him when she is in town.

BIANCA HARVEY
AUSTIN, TEXAS

Bianca is a beautiful white-and-black Lhasa Apso who has stolen our hearts with her looks and personality. When a puppy, she invented her own favorite, very wild and noisy game of attacking a large, empty plastic bottle. First she works at removing the label and lid, then rolls, throws, and chases it while she growls and barks. Often she's amazingly calm and spends hours on the seat of my sewing room's bay window, watching the world pass by. She is very loving with all the family, but does lots of barking out of sheer joy and excitement.

BILL ADLER
CHATSWORTH, CALIFORNIA

Bill, a black-and-white American Staffordshire Terrier, was born July 1, 1993. He is a family dog but is most devoted to his dad and best buddy, Ted. With a black spot over one eye, Bill looks almost as comical as he acts. He is always ready for a game, and his playful personality charms everyone in his midst. Bill's dream day is spent stream-walking with his dad, then out for hamburgers (he even eats the pickles!), followed up with a warm shower and towel-drying (his personal favorite). WHAT A DOG!

BIMBO NORONHA
GAITHERSBURG, MARYLAND

This Bimbo is anything but a dumb blond female. At any rate, he's not blond and he's not female. Actually, he's a male black Labrador. And he's no mental giant. But he makes up for it in the affection department. I brought him home in 1983 in the palm of my hand. He's put on about seventy pounds since then. Like all Labs, he loves the water but retrieves only balls and sticks although he'd prefer real ducks. He's crazy about pear cores, terrified of thunder and lightning, and enjoys squirming or sleeping on his back and having his chest and ears scratched.

BLAZE MONDARY
RISING SUN, INDIANA

Blaze is a nine-month-old, eighty-five-pound Golden Retriever. His registered name is Mondary's Blaze of Gold. He loves to swim in the Ohio River and fetch sticks. He will eat absolutely anything—especially tomatoes! He loves to roll on very dead things (catfish, etc.); he thinks he smells wonderful and doesn't understand why no one wants to pet him! He also loves to romp and play with kids. His favorite trick is "shake hands." Blaze bites at water coming out of a hose and jumps in the shower while we bathe! His best dog buddy is Sparky Mondary.

BLOM'S AUTUMN OF AUGUST
LAS VEGAS, NEVADA

She's a beautiful white/buff Cocker Spaniel who was born August 7, 1991, and came home with us at six weeks weighing three pounds (now twenty-six pounds—all feet, ears, feathers, and two-inch-long eyelashes). She loves to have her tummy rubbed, is very cuddly, and can melt your heart with her big, sad brown eyes. Favorite times are playing with her toys, pestering her sister Pandie, and pulling leaves and flowers off silk plants! She doesn't care for dog food at all, but loves peanut butter, Ritz crackers, and pizza.

BLUEBOY'S ISAAK
ROY, WASHINGTON

I saak's loyalty to his companion, Bill Hasemann, and to the Hasemann family is legend. His quiet, yet strong presence showcases the best traits of the breed Bouvier des Flandres. His physical and emotional strength is without equal, and he would protect his family at all costs. Yet Isaak is most happy sitting by (or on!) Bill's feet or when he can chase beetles in the river. He's the gentle leader of his pack, loving Roxy and Hanna, patiently caring for the others, carefully trying not to hurt Bentley. A dog for all seasons and for all Hasemanns.

BO GONICK
MANASQUAN, NEW JERSEY

Bo is a Maltese with flowing white hair, often adorned with bandanas and bows. Perhaps weighing all of seven pounds, Bo is literally afraid of his own shadow. Ask him about his nephew, Humphrey, and he trembles. Bo is sweet and precious, and loves to sit in a lap and be petted. At times, though, he will act tough, curl back his lips, and show his teeth. Bo enjoys long walks in the neighborhood and, in fact, once dragged home a steak bone bigger than himself. He loves car rides, his pastel bed, sleeping on Nettie's pillow, and watching television with Daddy.

BO BANDIT BRIGHTBILL
ROANOKE, VIRGINIA

Bo is an energetic six-year-old Collie/Shepherd mix. His peculiarities include urinating on unpleasant cuisine (peas) and his insatiable desire to chase cars. Bo boasts a four-foot vertical leap and approaches thirty miles per hour during pursuit. There was one occasion when he successfully subdued a good-natured motorist. Bo jumped through the driver's window, across the nice lady's lap and into the passenger's seat—ready to go for a ride! Bo is one loved mutt!

BOB RENDALL
DURHAM, NORTH CAROLINA

We knew Bob, a handsome Shepherd mix, for three years before he escaped from his abusive owners and we were finally able to adopt him from our local shelter. After undergoing heartworm treatment, he developed a near-fatal case of parvo virus, but survived thanks to the expert care and devotion of the doctors and staff at the Cornwallis Road Animal Hospital. An important family member, along with his dog sister Dutchess and his fourteen cat siblings, his daily routine includes washing Dutchess's face, enjoying Vie-de-France rolls, providing work for small appliance repairmen, and protecting us all from the ceiling fan.

BOLERO ("BO") CHISMAN
HAMPTON, VIRGINIA

This Border Collie's past is a mystery. I do know he chases cars, so we're training his "eye" for herding basketballs and catching frisbees. He's very good at both. He also stares at the cat a lot, which earns him several smacks a day (to a cat, staring is very fresh), and pushes the Golden around by licking his chin, which earns far fewer smacks than biting did. With people he is gentle—sometimes shy—but always willing to listen when I take the time to show him how.

BONNIE BELL BREE SPRINGSTUN
NEW YORK, NEW YORK

Bonnie is a beautiful Shetland Sheepdog, companion to Carol. Adopted at one year of age from a shelter, Bonnie has moved to New York's Central Park West, where she is known as "Little Lassie." Her serene daily walks in the park are marred only by her mysterious fear of horses. Bonnie's "Buddha-like" love and trust make her a very precious presence to all who see her on a daily basis and to those "harried" New York strangers who take a moment to meet her. May her message of love go on for many years.

BOOBOO BADOO
ST. CLOUD, MINNESOTA

Occupation: Tri-County Humane Society Mascot. BaDoo arrived at the shelter in January 1990, thin, dehydrated, and unable to stand. Two inches of his shoulder blade had been blown away by a shotgun. BaDoo was a model patient and adored his new people and surroundings. BaDoo's job as shelter mascot goes further than greeting customers and hanging out on his beanbag. He allows us to discuss the responsibilities of dog ownership and dispel myths that shadow the Doberman breed. BaDoo also supports us emotionally. Some days he is the only one to thank us for the work we do. That's okay—his sincerity is unsurpassed.

BOOBOO DEICHELBOR
MYRTLE BEACH, SOUTH CAROLINA

Booboo was a little black dog, about twenty-five pounds, with white on his muzzle, chest, and paws. He loved riding in the car when I did my errands. One day I was in a shop where he could see me through the windows. He had his paws on the steering wheel to see out and accidentally stood on the horn. I came running out of the shop to stop him, but he had learned a lesson. After that, when we took him with us and he thought we'd been gone too long, he would begin blowing the horn!

BORODIN LYNLOCH'S SILVERFIRE, CD CGC
CANDOR, NEW YORK

Dana is a rough blue merle Collie. He originally lived with Yuri Orlov, the world-renowned physicist, Soviet dissident, and human rights activist. Unfortunately, Dana derived too much pleasure from and created too much havoc by harassing the Orlovs' cats—now a long-gone fault that Dana blames on his having been a puppy at the time—and he found himself being adopted by a novice dog trainer. Not wanting to spend his entire life being shifted from home to home because of behavior problems, Dana learned some manners and made everyone proud by becoming his owner's first obedience-titled dog.

BOWSY AND TIPPY MOORE
FAIRBANKS, ALASKA

This brother-sister team was found abandoned one cold February day. Unwanted and abused puppies, they found a loving home where they live outdoors in an insulated doghouse. They have opposite personalities. A liberated female, Tippy detects any strange sound and barks immediately. Bowsy, still shy, is cautious and retiring. When they were puppies, Tippy showed her authority by holding Bowsy's hind leg in her mouth. Now top dog, Bowsy tolerates Tippy's hyperactivity and excessive friendliness. Their mistress appreciates their watchful care, especially when they alert her to interloping moose or foxes. These German Shepherd/Siberian Huskies make wonderful pet friends.

BRANDY BELONGIE
SUNRISE, FLORIDA

Brandy is an eleven-year-old Weimaraner. His average day starts out with an early morning snack followed by a nap. When he awakes, it is to go lounge by the pool to achieve maximum tannage. This exhausting activity is then followed by a nap. It is early evening when next he arises, and it is dinnertime. Dinner is followed by a stroll around the neighborhood and a nap. He awakes just in time for a bedtime biscuit and then settles down for the night in preparation for the next day's work.

BRANDY ALEXANDRIA JOHNSON
FRANKLIN, INDIANA

Brandy loves people and our horse. She runs the fence with him and tries to kick like he does. She loves Dairy Queen ice cream but thinks it comes from the microwave because I put it there to soften it. She barks "I love you," especially for a vanilla wafer. A light beige German Shepherd, with big, expressive brown eyes, she was born early in the morning on May 11, 1988. She wags her tail at everything and would rather be loved than eat. To Brandy, everything is new and a big adventure.

BRAT TROUT-JONES
ELKHART, INDIANA

To know him is to love him. Despite many serious operations and heart trouble, Brat keeps his love flowing to everyone he knows. Brat has and loves to wear his huge collection of bow ties, bandannas, sweaters, and a new bomber jacket that Santa Paws gave him last year for Christmas. Brat only recently stopped answering the telephone. He is so full of love that, except for his form and lack of voice, you would think he was human. Yes, to know him is to really love him.

70

BRONSON HAMMARLUND
FARMINGTON HILLS, MICHIGAN

My mother, Ardene Hammarlund, has always spoiled her children—both her human and her animal children. Her Lhasa Apso, Bronson, is a vegetarian. My mom goes to the grocery store every day and gets a salad for Bronson at the salad bar. She gives Bronson the salad in the car. When she parks the car in the garage, he stops eating his salad. He won't eat it in the house. So she keeps on driving until Bronson is all done with his salad!

BRUCE EAVERS
STAUNTON, VIRGINIA

Bruce is a nine-year-old yellow Lab. He loves to eat and has to be on a strict diet just to maintain his current weight of 112 pounds. Bruce is the family guard dog—a duty he takes very seriously. Strangers are not welcome until he is sure they are invited guests. Once this is established, he becomes very affectionate. Bruce lives near a campground and whenever possible sneaks away for a little camping excitement. He returns home a happy camper, leaving behind a hungry camper. Fortunately for Bruce, his daddy takes care of making amends with the campers. To know Bruce is to love him.

BRUNNHILDE HEIL HINISHUND
AMHERST, MASSACHUSETTS

A two-year-old miniature long-haired Dachshund, Brunnhilde sings "We're Off to See the Wizard, the Wonderful Wizard of Oz" from the movie *The Wizard of Oz*. A soprano as well as a munchkin, she can't (read: refuses to) sing any other song and loves (read: insists) singing it at all dinner parties.

BRUNO (REYES)
SHERMAN OAKS, CALIFORNIA

Bruno is our four-year-old Rottweiler/ Doberman. We call him The Lick Monster. If you've been welcomed into our home, Bruno sees to it that you're licked clean. You have only one chance to escape The Lick Monster and that is to show him a tennis ball. Where the ball goes, Bruno will follow. Then, when you're done, you can say, "Okay, Bruno, last one," and he will happily go lie down with his ball, leaving your saliva-covered body to dry.

BRUNZI MARANGONI
GARRISON, NEW YORK

Brunzi is a seven-year-old Golden Retriever whose favorite activities include visiting his elderly friends at a local nursing home, swimming with his sister "Chaos" and his girlfriend "Miss Gemma," eating frozen yogurt at Baskin Robbins with his other girlfriend "Zamora," and whiling away the hours snoozing in bed. An incorrigible chowhound, Brunzi happily helps himself to any food within snoot-reach and frequently has to wear a bib to control his drooling. Brunzi, named after his grandfather Dr. Bruno Marangoni, is himself a Ph.D. (perfectly happy dog)!

BRYDON GARONZIK-DIFONZO
PHILADELPHIA, PENNSYLVANIA

Brydie is a purebred male Beagle adopted as an adult by James and Sara. Though middle-aged, he has a pretty puppy face. Affectionate and demanding, he howls and weeps when we come home, whether we're gone two minutes or two days. His favorite sport is being chased up and down the halls while we scream "Where is my dog?" in falsetto voices. Other nicknames include Beej, Bugsey, Bugs-A-Mugs, Pooter, and That Boy-That Boy. Brydon is the subject of several songs we have written, including "Let's Go Houndin'," "(He's Justa) Brydon Pooter Boy," and "Do Da Dog Do Da Dog Doo?"

BUDDY
MORRISTOWN, NEW JERSEY

Buddy (1926–1938), a female German Shepherd, was the first Seeing Eye dog. Buddy was born in Switzerland, where she was trained to guide Morris Frank, a young blind American. On June 11, 1928, Morris Frank and Buddy arrived in New York City. The increased independence and mobility that Buddy provided Mr. Frank led to the founding of the Seeing Eye in 1929. Since then, the Seeing Eye, a philanthropy, has matched over 10,000 Seeing Eye dogs with blind people from all over the United States and Canada. In his lifetime, Mr. Frank had six Seeing Eye dogs, all German Shepherds named Buddy.

BUDDY WAYNE MYERS
EVANSVILLE, INDIANA

Buddy Wayne is an affectionate Sheltie who always greets us at the door with a leap into our arms. Whether he's wearing a potato-chip bag on his head, barking at unfamiliar posters on the wall, or prancing about in his red coat, he's never far away from Jerry, Karen, Jenna, and Jay, offering protection from things unknown to us in the human world. Buddy is also well liked in the neighborhood due to his courteous ways and his respect for living things. (He knows when and where to urinate.) Buddy Wayne's the best dog a family could ever have!

BUFFIE SUE SCHULTZ
ARLINGTON, TEXAS

Buffie is a twelve-year-old Cocker. Her favorite pastime is trying to carry all her toys at once to keep them away from her three sisters. She doesn't really mind sharing, but her sisters don't take as good care of her possessions as she would like. She loves to swim and retrieve her frog from the pool. Her greatest desire in life is to be an only dog.

BUFF'S MISS LIQUORICE
OVID, COLORADO

Liquorice was a beautiful black miniature French Poodle. We gave her to our ten-year-old daughter for her birthday. She (Liquorice, not the child) had one odd habit—she adored black olives! We would dry them and roll them across the family room floor and have fun watching her scramble across the tiles. She ate the fruit and dropped the pit daintily on the floor! She lived to be seventeen years of age. We miss her.

BUTTONS CAMPO
PUTNAM VALLEY, NEW YORK

Our rather large Shih Tzu has always been unconditionally devoted to our family, but most especially to Rob. Buttons was four when Rob was called home to his creator. On the day Rob was laid to rest, over 1,000 friends and family attended. Buttons journeyed to the cemetery later that afternoon with Rob's dad. Though never before having visited the cemetery, Buttons jumped from the car and made a beeline for Rob's final resting place. He lay there at the foot of Rob's grave as though having been summoned. Buttons is eight now and time has not dampened his devotion.

CAGNEY HAMBER
SEA CLIFF, NEW YORK

Cagney, a Silky Terrier, doesn't know she's a dog. She's a princess living in a castle overlooking the sea. Mornings, King John takes her for a stroll throughout the kingdom before he goes to slay dragons. Breakfast with the Queen Mum follows. Afternoons, there are lawn parties at the neighboring palace of Tess, a West Highland princess. Tina, her Lady-in-Waiting, serves delicious treats. Sir Lou, a brave knight, protects the princesses from menacing foreigners like German Shepherds, Irish Setters, and French Poodles! Princess Cagney is most happy, however, in the evening when the King throws a Ball.

CALLIE FLOWER BOREMAN
SMITHVILLE, OHIO

Callie Flower Boreman made her debut on November 25, 1980, the perfect mixture of Border Collie mother, Keltie and Collie father. Callie never tires of her favorite pastime—playing ball. Dad tosses and Callie leaps. Knowing Dad's a dentist, not an athlete, Callie obeys his command of "bring the ball closer" until the ball is within an inch of his grasp. Playing ball with her sister Roxanne, an Angora rabbit, was always a sight. Her new sister, Pickles the cat, isn't quite as enthusiastic, but Callie still tries to be friends. Callie does the best flea check and bedroom eyes of anyone.

CALLIOPEE'S CONSTELLATION
LAKE WORTH, FLORIDA

Calliopee is an eight-year-old Dalmatian. She prides herself on her complete collection of fashion headwear for different occasions throughout the year. The Statue of Liberty crown is her favorite! Her hobby is hunting chameleons with her cat friend, Bobby. Her latest endeavor is flipping her bowl when she feels she needs more food. Her pet peeves are thunderstorms and sleeping on the floor.

CARLY SIMON GRANDPAP JR. HAGE (A.K.A. BISCUIT)
SAN DIEGO, CALIFORNIA

Biscuit is a blond three-and-a-half-year-old, thirty-five-pound Cocker Spaniel. We adopted this adorable, loving, brown-eyed puppy when he was one and a half. He thinks he's one of the cats (climbs on anything he can reach). He loves all things edible (pizza and diet Coke are favorites) and some inedible (teeth retainers—$180 worth). He chews bubble gum, too! He loves riding in the car. He barks at the doorbell (even on TV). He's very affectionate and licks everyone to death. And, believe it or not, he understands and speaks Spanish—just ask our cleaning lady!

CASABLANCA LIEBERMAN
PLANTATION, FLORIDA

Cassie is a fifteen-pound (on a light day) ... umm ... mixed breed. She came into our lives as a two-pound Chihuahua and mutated into a much larger species. Her joy in life is eating, and she decided at an early age that she would play with each and every piece of kibble before eating it. Sometimes the food is possessed by an evil force that talks to Cassie, and she will pummel the food until there is not a trace left of the evil spirit. Mealtime leaves Cassie exhausted, so a nap is definitely next on her agenda.

CASEY ANDREWS
DURHAM, NORTH CAROLINA

Casey is a three-year-old chocolate Lab. Casey is very sociable and thinks she is supposed to be included in all of our activities. If she is excluded, she gets very vocal. One night last winter we walked over to our neighbor's house to visit. Casey watched us go and barked her displeasure. After a few hours, the doorbell rang several times. It was very late, and our neighbors could not imagine who could be at the door. When they turned on the porch light, there stood Casey on her hind legs, ringing the bell and looking in the window for us.

CASSANDRA USTANIK
LANSING, ILLINOIS

C assie is a four-year-old black Miniature Schnauzer who goes to work every day with her owners. With over eighty employees there, she gets lots of love and attention. She always lets her owners know if someone who doesn't belong is on the premises. Cassie's favorite pastimes are eating and sleeping, but she loves playing with her stuffed animals and chewing on dirty socks. She has an in-ground pool in her backyard that she will have nothing to do with because she hates water. In fact, it would be quite traumatic if she would have to step in a puddle!

CATTLE KATE'S COWBOY CODY LOCH
FAIRVIEW HEIGHTS, ILLINOIS

Cody, an Australian Cattle Dog, is my pride and joy. He has boundless energy and an outgoing personality. As a member of a military family, Cody is a seasoned traveler. He has lived in the state of Washington and currently lives in Illinois. His favorite activities include playing fetch, going for walks, playing with his older brother Euchre, taking naps and, of course, snacking on dog biscuits. Intelligent, loyal and affectionate—my canine companion Cody is all this and more!

CHADRIK MAN OF WAR VON CRISA ("ANGUS")
RENO, NEVADA

Angus is a "handsome hunk of a man." He is a massive buff Rottweiler with the demeanor and facial expressions of a teddy bear. He brings so much joy and laughter to me, as well as the patients he visits with on his pet therapy assignment at a local hospital. The Angee-Man's favorite passions are stealing anything he can get his lips on, paperwork, and cuddling. He also harasses his mate, Amber, by continuously wrestling and caressing her. Angus spends his down time upside down and snoring. Angus is true, noble, and a very loyal Rottweiler. I am truly proud to have him in my life.

CHAMPION ARLAND'S SUN MAIDEN ("MANDI")
SANTA BARBARA, CALIFORNIA

March 11, 1976–May 15, 1991. Proclaimed by respected judges to be an ideal representation of the Shetland Sheepdog, my beautiful Mandi, a gift to me at sixteen, proved to be my teenage dream come true. Together, as a hard to beat team, Mandi became my first champion, highlighting her illustrious show career by the title of Best Female Sheltie in the Nation, 1980. Working partners and best friends, we understood each other completely. Though devilish at times, for fifteen years my "Angel" was the first and last lovely vision I'd see each day. She lived for more food, more walks, and more me.

CHANCE RIOUX
ELLINGTON, CONNECTICUT

C hance, badge #9015, served proudly as a patrol dog for the Connecticut State Police, graduating on September 12, 1983. He and his partner, Sgt. Wayne Rioux, were the first team assigned to the State Police Tactical Team, performing with distinction in this dangerous position for two years. On May 16, 1985, Chance and his partner were certified as a narcotics detection team. Chance and Sgt. Riuox made 72 felony arrests and 44 misdemeanor arrests, and located 10 missing persons. Chance died September 17, 1990, leaving behind Wayne, Denise, Chad, and Bryan, who greatly miss him.

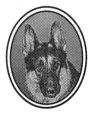

CHAOS ("BALLY") MARANGONI
GARRISON, NEW YORK

haos is a five-year-old Golden Retriever who suffers from a tennis ball obsession. She will fetch tirelessly (for bally), swim endlessly (to retrieve bally), and obey every command (when bribed with bally). She lives with her Golden Retriever brother Brunzi and two cats (dog toys). She and her brother look forward to summer vacations at doggie camp each year in Vermont (of course her favorite activity is flyball). Chaos will catch *every* tennis ball thrown at her, no matter how many or at what speed, and aspires to someday be featured on David Letterman's "stupid pet tricks."

CHARLEMAGNE DE STUART
STUART, FLORIDA

Charlie is a Poodle and weighs twelve pounds. His color is café au lait, and his nose and eyes are the same shade. His ears are full and magnificent (he must have passed twice when they were giving them out). He loves everyone—people, dogs, cats, and birds. When my husband leaves the house for a trip, Charlie knows he will telephone so he sits at the phone until he does. To me, he is one of God's special blessings.

CHARLES S. DICKENS
CEDAR RAPIDS, IOWA

Charlie is a ten-month-old Old English Sheepdog. He is a herder from sunup to sundown. Weighing eighty pounds, he'll push, shove, and nip until you're in the corner. He is very loving and wants hugs while on your lap. Charlie's nickname is Sewer Pipe Wilson—due to digging, rutting in the mud, and playing with the hose. He's a mess most of the time, and we love him dearly. His favorite pastimes are catch and fetch. He's good, considering the heavy fur coat and his size. Unlike his namesake, he can't write novels, but we are hopeful. He is our "Christmas Carol."

CHARLIE, THE EX-CAIRN
CHESTERFIELD, MISSOURI

D riven to crime by a diet of Fit-N-Trim, our overweight Cairn Terrier, Charlie, was brought to our door by a policeman accompanied by a very hassled lady. It seems Charlie, several times, had partaken of her cat's food left out on her patio. She mentioned she had had a bad day and just couldn't take the pilfering of Fluffy's Fancy Feast anymore. My husband, who had had an equally bad day, pointed out to her that cat food can be harmful to dogs and should not be left outside. Mr. Policeman decided it was not a beautiful day in the neighborhood and cited us for violating the leash law.

CHATFIELD JJ SHA'MER (SHAE)
CHATFIELD, TEXAS

S hae, a Great Pyrenees, always showed the regal bearing of being a keeper. When a calf was born, Shae would bury the afterbirth, then lie close by the new calf as the mother grazed. He chose our garden as his retreat, yet would always be on guard keeping peace. Our Lord must have needed him for keeping—Sha'mer is a name from the Bible ("Keeper"). Our Gentle Giant faithful companion will always be remembered with loving respect.

CHAUNCEY
SAN ANTONIO, TEXAS

Chauncey is a West Highland Terrier with a very diverse appetite. During his life he has eaten a two-pound bag of jalapeño corn bread mix, a tube of zinc oxide, and a can of chocolate Slim Fast. All three episodes resulted in trips to the vet and luckily all had happy endings. Once he was lost and ended up in a stranger's home seven miles away, seated on top of the master bedroom bed on a feather pillow. The owner of the home came home and found him there. She called the number on his tag and he was rescued.

CHELSEA CHRISTOPHER
PINOLE, CALIFORNIA

Chelsea is a beautiful and loving GIANT Schnauzer. Chelsea loves to go for rides in *her* truck, especially up to Reno to see her sister. She has been known to bark all the way there, too. Chelsea's favorite times are spent booffing and stomping her toys, tripping people on the way to the telephone, and snoring so loud that no one else can sleep. When it's hot, Chelsea loves to take a dip in her pool and fling wet mung from her beard on everyone. After her dip in the pool, she likes to go to the beauty shop.

CHELSEA HOUSEHOLDER
LAKE ST. LOUIS, MISSOURI

Chelsea is a one-and-a-half-year-old Chesapeake and Labrador Retriever. We installed a Dutch door to confine her to the kitchen. She didn't like that, so she ate the linoleum down to the wood. Next week she pulled the kitchen curtains down and slept on them. Thanksgiving she ate the pumpkin pie (cooling on the counter). Chelsea spotted a squirrel, leaped out the window, and hit her head on the curbside mailbox; she recovered well from the head concussion. She can't relate to her mirrored image and gets depressed. Chelsea thinks she's a person. She may need therapy.

CHELSEY "BELSEY" VAUGHN
GLENGORA, CALIFORNIA

Chelsey's a five-year-old Cocker Spaniel with freckles across her nose. She and her brother Winston are inseparable. Chelsey's the cuddly one. Her favorite spot is on my lap, hiding her face under my arm. Winston is the bossy one. But one day Chelsey got back at him. Winston was getting into the trash can. Chelsey, knowing he was being "bad," came running to me. She sat quickly, looking at me with those big brown eyes that said, "Mom, come look at what Winston's getting into!" With her help I was able to catch him red-handed.

CHELSEA MCSORLEY WADE
LONG BEACH, MISSISSIPPI

Chelsea is an adorable Sheltie/Shepherd mix who loves to play. She especially enjoys "wrestling" with her human daddy, Merrill. As in the World Wrestling Federation matches shown on television, the opponents are announced and Chelsea immediately starts barking! The action gets lively as Chelsea and Merrill exchange elbow drops and blasts to the chest. When Merrill pretends to have been knocked unconscious by one of her blows, Chelsea revives him by licking his face. Her sweetness and sense of fun make her a much-loved member of the Wade family.

CHELSEA SCHOEPP
SCHAUMBURG, ILLINOIS

Chelsea, a blue Merle Shetland Sheepdog born September 7, 1992, is a very active little girl who loves to go for walks, play frisbee, and fetch her ball. Her inside activities include rolling over and sharing her rawhide bones with her cat friend Romeo. When she's bored, she will pull out all of her favorite toys; and she is just learning how to put them away. Although she does chase our cats, she doesn't have a mean bone in her body. The one thing that she is the best at is making even the grumpiest person smile.

CHELSEA WILLIAMS
JONESBOROUGH, TENNESSEE

Chelsea is a two-year-old Pekingese who loves to watch television. She barks at horses, race cars, and "fingerman" commercials. Sometimes her mom and dad, Carolyn and Tom, have to change the channel. Chelsea loves stuffed animals and has quite a collection. She is afraid of riding in a car, but she loves to go visit her cousin Jessie. Although she chases and barks at birds, Chelsea is fearful of flies and will leave the room when one is around.

CHICO HABERCHAK
APOLLO, PENNSYLVANIA

Seventeen years old, Chico is a black-and-white male Terrier mix in the dusk of his life. He enjoys lying in a sunny spot on the deck or looking out the patio doors to watch the deer feed beneath the apple tree. In the winter, his favorite spot is in front of the fireplace. Although he is now hard of hearing, he can still hear a piece of candy being unwrapped in the other room.

CHICO MARTINI GONZALES IVERSON
BOWIE, MARYLAND

Chico is a gentle and friendly Chihuahua who loves life, people, and nature. He adores sunbathing on his porch while snoozing. Every day is a new day for this happy little fellow. He smells flowers, plays with butterflies, and saves turtles by alerting his friends. On holidays, Chico dresses up and prances around showing off his costumes. His favorite outfit is Uncle Sam, on the Fourth of July. This pooch loves posing for pictures—a ham at heart who loves pampering. At a community dog show, bagpipes started to play and Chico chimed in, singing proudly. Scotch he's not, loved he is.

CHIPPY LAUDET
NEW YORK CITY, NEW YORK

Chippy is a gray-and-white Puli. Born in March 1979, he is the consummate East Villager—sporting purple hair in his punk period—with class to boot! His mischievous and tail-wagging enthusiasm have delighted everyone as far away as France, where he visits his grandparents. Chippy's a great watchdog—he watches canine activity on the block from the comfort of his armchair by the window. His favorites include girl dogs, garbage, licking himself, and playing on the bed. Chippy has a storm and a star named after him, small tokens of the boundless love he inspires.

CHIPS (FROM THE DENBY LOG STAFF) WINTER
DETROIT, MICHIGAN

Before he was a year old, this joyful Sheltie went to college with his mother, staying in a motel and eating at the same drive-in for eight weeks. Chips admired the cows and horses on the twenty-mile drive to the university and sat behind the wheel for the three hours of class time. Back home, Chips loved to run through the sprinkler, sit close to his owner, ride with hair flying in their convertible, and amuse kids on Halloween in his bluebird costume. Best of all, dishwashing was interrupted so every one could come and watch Lassie. Fifteen years of joy!

CHY-NA CHECKER OUT (MAR-BOL) POWELL
PARMA, OHIO

Chy-Chy is a three-year-old Siberian Husky who loves splashing in her swimming pool all summer, but come the first snow she's looking for her harness. Chy-Chy is small (thirty-two pounds), silver and white, with one blue eye and one brown eye. A sled dog all her life, she ran in the wheel position until the 1992–93 season, when she was made a lead dog. Chy-Na looks quite smart in her royal blue harness.

CIAO IV WINGFIELD
KANSAS CITY, MISSOURI

Ciao is a nine-year-old cinnamon Chow Chow male. He has two human companions, Wes and Laura, and three dog companions, his son Yi Tian and two Scottie sisters, Ceilidh and Nessie. Ciao is the patriarch of the pack. He enjoys wrestling with his son and ministering to the Scotties' needs. He is a terrific watchdog and loving friend. He is especially fond of raw cauliflower. When begging for food, he holds to the Chow Chow rule of three: 1) It smells, 2) It is his color, or 3) Humans are eating it.

CINDY OLSON
COLTON, CALIFORNIA

Cindy is a twelve-year-old Pomeranian who knows which car to get into when asked to go for a ride. After dinner she follows my husband into the TV room and looks at the cupboard and whirls around until he gives her a jellybean (licorice not accepted). Then sometimes she tries to get a second jellybean, and you have to show her your open hands so that she knows you are onto her trick. Similarly, if she does not get a taste of Coca-Cola at night, she stands in front of you until you get her some. These things go on daily.

CINNAMON VERSIGA
DALLAS, TEXAS

On one of our visits to the humane society to "just look," Cinnamon, a five-month-old Chow, gave us a look we couldn't pass up. She's been a perfect family addition since she came home with us that day. She is an affectionate and loyal companion who enjoys having her belly rubbed. She loves chasing any critter that will run from her, unless it's a skunk—then she retreats with a sample of nature's perfume! Cinnamon and her sister Shastah love to go on trips. Whether across the field or across the state, Cinnamon is the consummate EXPLORER.

CLEOPATRA BURKE
PUTNAM VALLEY, NEW YORK

Strong and purest Golden . . . Devoted till the end . . . Patient and proud . . . A sympathetic friend . . . Gave up Manhattan for the good life in the woods . . . Fearful of nothing, except vacuums and Chinese food . . . Fond of soccer balls, big red vans, and animals that fly . . . "Fetch till you drop" is the motto she lives by . . . Swimmer of all waters, oceans, streams, and trenches . . . In search of the world's most nauseating stenches . . . A moody princess who can't look you in the eye . . . She lives and loves only for her special guy.

COCOA FREEMAN
KUTZTOWN, PENNSYLVANIA

Cocoa is a fifteen-year-old Peke-A-Poo who is extremely agile and active for his age. This is due to the arrival of Samantha the Bulldog five years ago and Spirit the Bichon this year. Cocoa has an exceptional personality and everyone knows him. For a dog who is 100-plus in human years, he really has his wits about him—he still knows where his old girlfriends live!

COCOA HLAVATY
CHICAGO, ILLINOIS

Cocoa appears to be somewhat of a Shepherd/Afghan mix. She was found in a shelter after being a stray. Initially very shy, she has established herself as queen of the house (although she still spooks easily). She loves to play with her Chewman and will fetch him, or her frisbee, or Kong, etc. She is a momma's girl, and loves to be near people. She now has a new stepbrother whom she loves to tease and play with. Now if I could just keep them out of my flowers!

CODY QUINN
MIRA LOMA, CALIFORNIA

Cody's fourteen years (1978–1992) could fill this book. She was the ultimate companion, farm dog, watchdog, and friend to Lacy J. She loved riding in her truck, playing ball, and lying in the sun. She loved people and thought everyone who visited came to see her. I still see the sweet look on her face when I would come home from work. Cody was always there and never let me down. She never got old, just regal. I miss her so much, and I know she misses me.

COMMISSIONER RANDOLF ("TUFFY") BEMAN
PONTE VEDRA, FLORIDA

Tuffy (the Tuff-Stuff, the Tuffmeister) is a gentleman of impeccable character and dignity. Born October 30, 1982, Tuffy has crisscrossed the United States many times, finally assembling enough frequent-flyer points to bring along Dixie Belle, the joy and bane of his life. His most memorable flight occurred between Hartford and Denver. Enticed by the prospect of freedom and odors of food service, he escaped the in-cabin kennel to wander down several rows of seats while his master crawled among passenger ankles to retrieve him. His capture was greeted by applause, relief, and a standing "O"!

117

COOKIE ("KOOKIE") OSBORN
BROOMFIELD, COLORADO

At three, Cookie is the youngest of our three retired Greyhound race dogs, although she looks like the oldest. She retired at the age of one and a half years because of an occasional inability to focus on the race (she was known to sit down in the middle of the track when confused); when she tried, though, her trainers say she was unbeatable. For about a year after retiring, she was afraid of *everything*. Lately, however, since she's been focusing on being a pet, she has again been unbeatable. Cookie is as shy as a lunar eclipse and as sweet as a lilac.

CORGI BUDD
VERBANK, NEW YORK

Corgi is a Pembroke Welsh Corgi one and a half years old, who is clearly the world's greatest dog. His hobbies include walking on furniture, begging for food, playing frisbee, and taking rides in the car. He loves cheeseburgers from McDonalds and stuffs the pickles behind the seats with his paw. Corgi also has a sensitive side; he comes running when he hears the word "ow" and he hates to see anyone cry. Among all these other attributes, he is also very well dressed. His favorite outfit is a black T-shirt that says PAIN IN THE NECK and that quickly sums up his whole personality.

CRACKERS SPENHOFF
FRESNO, CALIFORNIA

This little tan dog from the SPCA
Stole my heart one bright sunny day.
I named her Crackers and off we went
On a journey of love I'll never forget.
With her by my side I finally found
What God said to be true, that love has no bounds.

Sixteen years have passed since that bright
sunny day,
Now God's called you back and with Him you
will stay.
Although in my heart you'll always be near,
Life still feels empty because you're not here.
When I get to heaven you'll be waiting for me,
Together again for all eternity.

CRYSTAL LYNN HERZOG
AVONDALE, ARIZONA

Crystal is six and a half years old. She is a golden Lab, but she is more red than golden. Crystal is a basketball fan. The only ball that she will play with is a miniature basketball; no other ball will do. When she can't find her ball, she goes into a panic attack, frantically searching the whole house and backyard, which eventually leads to everyone looking for her ball. Crystal also is a flashlight nut. She will attack the light on the ground from a flashlight—it's the wildest thing you've ever seen. All in all, Crystal is a very loving dog and lots of fun.

CUFFEE MACDONALD
WESTPORT, MASSACHUSETTS

C uffee, a four-year-old black Cocker Spaniel, is a Therapy Dog. Representing Jeff's Companion Animal Shelter, she makes pet-facilitated therapy visits to nursing homes, hospitals, and schools. Cuffee is not only a friendly giver of love but also a warm and gentle receiver of affections as she visits the residents in nursing homes and hospitals. She brings a smile, friendly memory, and a feeling of warmth to those who have been removed from animal contact and miss the love and affection she provides.

DAKOTA RAE SCHULZ
ARLINGTON, TEXAS

Dakota is a two-year-old, sixty-pound Lab/ Chow. She is the youngest of three sisters and is our pound puppy. Her idea of a chew stick is a log for the fireplace. Her favorite pastime is swimming with her Grand Mawmaw. Every day at exactly five-thirty, there she waits on the first step leading to the pool. She thinks her mother (who is really her sister) is a fourteen-pound Schnauzer. Whenever she is afraid, she tries to hide behind her. You can imagine how funny that looks.

DANCER SCRUFFLE SCHIFLER
NORTH RIDGEVILLE, OHIO

Scruff is a one-year-old, five-pound blue-and-gold female Yorkshire Terrier. She keeps her hair cut in a puppy-clip since she's so playful and doesn't want it all ratted up. Scruffy gets the most enjoyment attacking (playfully growling and nipping at) our heels and shoes as we walk. Shoes that don't move don't interest her. When Scruff sleeps, about a quarter-inch of her tongue sticks out of her mouth. Beware—don't chew an ice cube around her or she will bark and growl until she is given one of her own.

DAPHNE BEACH
MILLBROOK, NEW YORK

D aphne, better known as Peewee, hails from the heart of Brooklyn but now cools her fuzzy heels in horse country—the rolling hills of Dutchess County, New York. Peewee is a seven-month-old Cairn Terrier whose favorite thing in life (besides long walks and mealtimes) is chasing tiny toads through the wet grass. She loves other animals, especially cats, and is adept at going upstairs; she cannot, however, get back down, which results in a great many howls reverberating through the house. Daphne can usually be found in a snoozing heap with her two siblings (a Westie and a longhaired kitten) wherever the sun hits the rug.

DAVID
HEBBRONVILLE, TEXAS

David was a handsome cow dog who followed the chuckwagon at the ranch. He moved to Beeville with the Hause family. The children would teach him tricks and dress him in their clothes to play. He was a wonderful pal. One day the children were playing outside and young Daryl climbed into a discarded refrigerator. Mother wanted everyone in the car to go to Grandma's house, but this great dog kept barking and would not budge. Finally Mother went over and opened the refrigerator door. There was Daryl, safe and "hiding," unaware of the danger she could have been in.

DILLY EVANS
LAKELAND, FLORIDA

Dilly is a lively Papillon dog whose lovable personality demands your affection, although she's not always the perfect house guest. She likes to tell you about everything she sees, even if you don't want to hear it. Whenever it's treat time you can be sure Dilly will be in the front row, although she is a picky eater. She thinks it's great fun to hop in bed with you at night, and if you're not careful she'll pick her spot first—then you will have to make the best of the situation.

DING-A-LING FREUNDLICH
SHORT HILLS, NEW JERSEY

Born in 1976 and abandoned at six months because she wasn't a perfect Pekingese, Ling was rescued. This eight-pound, gremlin look-alike became the first mascot of St. Hubert's Giralda Animal Welfare and Education center in Madison, New Jersey. Her ten-year career brought smiles to more than 100,000 schoolchildren and nursing home residents. The Delta Society named her "Therapy Animal of the Year" in 1990. During her pampered retirement days, Ling slept on any of three beds, one heated. Meals were warmed perfectly and evenings were spent napping on my husband's chest or sweaty clothes. We'll miss her.

DINKUM COBBER FIELDS
ANDERSON, INDIANA

Dinkum Cobber is an Australian Shepherd born of Dingo and Sheila. She has one blue eye and one brown eye. Her name is a colloquialism: Dinkum means "true" and Cobber means "friend." She is the embodiment of the definition. After surviving an enigmatic disease from which she nearly perished and which caused her hair to fall out, she still believes that she merits the "people" food that was prepared for her during her illness. She shepherds the other two dogs away from her mistress to get all the attention, yet she has learned not to confront the cat.

DINO COOPER
HILLSIDE, ILLINOIS

Dino, at the age of seven, has become a fierce hunter. The part Beagle breed in him becomes apparent when he tracks down and kills his prey—Dino hunts flies in our house. His girlfriend, Tosha, comes over on her own whenever the gates are left open. Dino is a real ladies' man and will go to any extent to protect women. He has our neighbor trained. He will go to the fence and bark until the neighbors pet him. Dino can tell time. Every night at 7 P.M. without fail he will let Dad know it is time for Dino's treat.

DIVINE WILL BERKMAN
NEW YORK CITY, NEW YORK

Divine Will is a fourteen-year-old black Dachshund/Corgi mix who was adopted eight years ago, on Christmas Eve, from the ASPCA. Each year, on the Feast of St. Francis, Willie gets decked out in his best scarf to go to the Blessing of the Animals at St. John the Divine. He sleeps a lot now, as old guys do, and he's happiest when wrapped in his favorite rug, which he accomplishes by taking a corner in his teeth and rolling over twice. At walktime or mealtime he just rolls in the opposite direction.

DIXIE ANN PARKINSON
BLANCO, TEXAS

Dixie Anne is the newest addition to our family. She is a five-month-old shorthaired Chihuahua. She is fawn-colored and has long legs and *big* ears. She loves to play with her two sisters or with anyone else who is around. She will completely empty the toy box in a matter of minutes and have the toys all over the house. She moves anything not nailed down: she has the jaws of a hundred-pound dog (she weighs four pounds). We have also just discovered that she has found some way to get up on and rearrange Daddy's desk.

DIXIE BELLE BEMAN
PONTE VERDE, FLORIDA

Born October 26, 1990, Dixie Belle (a.k.a. The Dixinator and Dixie-Pixie) is an unbridled bundle of joy. It is said it's impossible to be unhappy around her, for she surrounds all with unquestioning love and affection. Her favorite pursuit is chameleon patrol on her sunny Florida back porch. Her most famous close call came when she consumed an entire package of fireplace matches, accidentally igniting one and burning a small hole in the rug! She has only to bat her beautiful black lashes to be forgiven every sin.

DOBIE WHEELER WALL
MILWAUKEE, WISCONSIN

Dobie, the Gentle Ben of red female Dobermans, has been a nanny to Jennifer since her September 1990 birth and serves as her surrogate pony. She had eighteen children, one of whom—Dylan—lived with her until his untimely death by the car of an inattentive driver. Dobie, who should be "terrible," spends half her day nudging someone for rubs and the other half divided between sleeping and stealing food from Jennifer. Anyone never realizing a Doberman can be lovable should meet Dobie. Aside from an occasional chewed rug, she is perfect. There will never be another one like her.

DOC HAMBY
CHARLOTTE, NORTH CAROLINA

In May of 1981 Doc caught the Goodyear Blimp. Most dogs chase cars and bark at tires. Doc caught the Blimp. It happened near the Charlotte Motor Speedway when the Blimp tried to land in our pasture. Doc decided that this thing was too close to his cows. He took off after it and caught the tether rope about five feet off the ground. He grabbed and shook it for all he was worth. The Blimp started to rise and Doc dropped off, but chased and barked after it. Doc retired after that and lived a contented life to age eleven. He was half Lab and half Irish Setter.

DOMINGO FRISCH
PINE GROVE, CALIFORNIA

D omingo is a black fourteen-year-old half Chow, half Wolf. We have had him for approximately ten years. He loves the snow. It's great for him to run through it, but he won't let me ride my tube down the hill. He pulls my sleeves and pant legs. If that won't work, he sits in front of me. He acts about sixty years old except when he hears the word "bye-bye"; then he is three years old. We love him.

DONNA'S CHRISTMAS EVE, CD
FAIR LAWN, NEW JERSEY

Chrissy is a female Miniature Schnauzer born November 22, 1991. She earned her Companion Dog title in February 1994 and passed the Canine Good Citizen test the next May. Big, expressive eyes, natural ears and a great personality have won her many modeling jobs for collars, heartworm preventive, and dog sweaters and jackets. Chrissy is a real sweetheart. Full of energy, she good-naturedly controls her siblings and occasionally takes time out to help raise orphaned kittens.

DOUGHBOY
WALTHAM, MASSACHUSETTS

D oughboy was a German Shepherd who belonged to D.A.R. Regent Nellie B. King. During World War I, the U.S. Army recruited him to be trained to provide messenger service. He successfully carried messages across the enemy line to our American troops. Doughboy became the first decorated War Dog. He returned home, where he lived a good life and eventually died of old age. He was buried in a mausoleum with his medals on display.

DUCHESS MAGGIE-MAY BERANEK
TAMPA, FLORIDA

Maggie-May, a three-year-old Yorkshire Terrier, rules the Beranek household. She's loud, pesky, curious, intelligent, often grumpy, and spoiled rotten. She has an opinion about everything: where the cat should sleep, dinnertime, walktime, playtime, and bedtime. Loves riding in the car, playing ball (her favorite), picnics, broccoli, giving kisses, exploring new places, and getting presents. Hates grooming, loud voices, being left behind, rainy days, and cats. She's six pounds of love and tenacity, with soft brown eyes and a heart as big as she is. My life is blessed because of her. She is a gift from God.

DUKE FORSTER
DEERFIELD BEACH, FLORIDA

Duke Forster is a brown-and-tan Yorkshire, eight pounds of terrier born in Florida. He is like a mole and likes to wrap himself under blankets, which he carries around with a bone larger than he is. He loves toys. I taught him to show me his teeth, and he will do it on command. Duke's favorite friend is a Boxer, and Duke can't wait to run and kiss his friend, who sits down. When it's bedtime, my husband calls him and he gets his bone, goes back to get his blanket, and goes to bed. He makes us laugh.

DUKE GARCIA
CHEVERLY, MARYLAND

The Duke of Cheverly is a beautiful male Golden Retriever, eight years young. He is extremely intelligent and very affectionate. When you say hello, he presents his paw to be shaken, and he also opens the gate for you when needed. Some of his pastimes are frisbee and ball-catching, gardening (picking green beans and raspberries are his favorite), and frolicking with other dogs. His favorite games are guessing which hand the ball is in and rolling the ball back and forth. At snack time he peels the bananas for everyone, but cheese and pepperoni are his favorite.

DUKE O'ROCKFORD
(ROCKY J. DOG)
LA CRESCENTA, CALIFORNIA

Rocky is a five-year-old, seventy-pound Dalmatian (black and white). He is not very friendly toward people or strange dogs, but he is very protective of his little brother Marty (a Dachshund) and he absolutely adores cats. Rocky is such a calm, passive dog that sometimes we have to make sure he's still breathing. Rocky loves to wiggle around on his back in the grass, play with his squeaky toys, give the cat a bath, and go for car rides.

DUKE RAMSETH
PORTLAND, OREGON

Some folks will say, "He's only a dog."
But those who know him have said,
"He's just as human as anyone,
And smarter than some well read."
He thinks he is cute when he does something
   smart;
Likes praise when he does as he's told.
He's easily hurt and so downcast
When he does something wrong and I scold.
He's been a good dog and is aging fast.
You see he is past eleven.
If you never knew him in this life,
You will probably meet him in heaven.

DUKE REDDING
SEQUIM, WASHINGTON

D uke is a Terrier/Poodle mix whom we adopted along with his mother when he was six weeks old. He has put much effort into training us to throw frisbees for him. He also enjoys playing hide-and-seek and seeing his owners act silly. He especially likes banking days, because at the drive-up window he gets to withdraw a dog biscuit anytime we make a deposit. The bank tellers in this town are all dog lovers as well. Duke has made our retirement years really special.

DUTCHESS ANNE LARSEN
IRON STATION, NORTH CAROLINA

Dutchess is a beautiful white longhaired German Shepherd. She acts very feminine, but you don't want to turn your back if she doesn't know you. She is eleven years old and extremely loyal and devoted to us. Dutchess loves to ride in the back of our truck. She can't jump in over the side anymore, so we give her a hand. Dutchess is never without a rock in her mouth. Her ground-down teeth are proof. She can catch a frisbee, but if you're not looking she will chew out the middle. Dutchess has been a wonderful friend.

DYLAN ELKES
TAMPA, FLORIDA

Dylan is a two-year-old Dalmatian Coach Hound. Although Dylan is a beautiful dog to look at, part of his charm is that he is somewhat ungraceful and slow in his movements. Dylan's favorite toy is a black plastic rat named Grover that he mothers. Even his companion dog, Daisy, isn't allowed to play with Grover. Dylan loves his backyard and does many "border" patrols a day to ensure nothing happens on his turf without his permission. Dylan is fond of Daisy and likes to spend much of his day playing with her.

EASY (PIE) ALEXANDER
NEW-SKY, NORTH CAROLINA

Easy is like no other. Her eyes speak. Her love is unconditional and her tail is absent. The Ease "be there" with her high fashion sense and acquired taste for people foods. She's marched in parades, sat in on college classes, and brought joy, warmth, and tenderness to those in need as a Pet Therapy companion. She's also loyal and courageous, unafraid to chase even the big dogs from her turf. When she was a pup, she looked like a Brillo pad. She's now grown up to be a beautiful brown-eyed girl, but she'll always be my baby, sweet Easy.

EBONY'S SHADOW, CGC, TDI
OREGON, OHIO

Shad, born June 1, 1992, is an eight-pound black Pomeranian with big, beautiful eyes and a warm, loving, laid-back personality. His brother, Ebony, selected him from his litter and helps train him in obedience. We affectionately call him "Piglet" because he's so roly-poly and makes a pigpen of himself and the house. When he was four months old, we began taking him along with the K-9's & Co. Therapy Dog group and developing an extensive costume wardrobe for him. We've trained him to pull a wagon filled with "treats" to pass out at children's shows.

ELVIS TRINIDAD
SAN MATEO, CALIFORNIA

ELVIS IS ALIVE! He was born late in August 1992 and was adopted in November. He is a Doberman/Hound mix male. He has Doberman markings but has the size, ears, tail, and personality of a Hound. We named him Elvis because he cries all the time (just like the song). His favorite time of day is when we go to the dog exercise area, where he has lots of friends and a few girlfriends. He loves his frisbee and toys, but most of all he likes stealing toys from other dogs and having them chase him.

EMILY KOFOS
TUCSON, ARIZONA

Emily, a red-and-white Beagle now one and a half years old, is a canine metal detector. Since I got her at six weeks old, she has dug up more than 200 nails in my backyard. These are not visible—they are underground. Emily smells them and digs and digs until she finds one. She then brings it in the house and gives it to me, usually not too willingly. Needless to say, my backyard looks like I have a large family of moles living there!

EMMA DEE O MISTY RIDGE
CAWLEY
UPPER MARLBORO, MARYLAND

Emma is a "wide open" two-year-old German Shepherd. She is still learning the ropes and enjoying her life to the fullest. Emma loves to eat popcorn, catching each kernel in midair. She also loves to play with our cat Russell. They are great buddies. Russell will attack her ankles, whereupon Emma will fling Russell on his back, pin him down with her massive paw, and ever so gently preen him from head to toe. Then Russell will somehow break free and scurry around the house with Emma in hot pursuit.

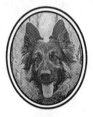

EMMETT ("MR. E") PEARSON
PLYMOUTH, MICHIGAN

When we first saw his little black face, black whiskers, gold eyes, and plume-like tail through the bars of his cage, we knew we just had to let him own us. We adopted seven-month-old Emmett from the Humane Society. He is our black Retriever. Emmett will fetch toy mice and other items like a shot when they are chucked across a room. He rockets four feet into the air in pursuit of his favorite prey, his flying feathered "bird" on a stick. "Air Emmett" shares two homes with us. He summers on Nantucket. Emmett is loved.

ERIC VON BRIDSONHAUS
FOREST PARK, GEORGIA

E
ric was a black-and-tan miniature Dachshund. He loved to retrieve tennis balls and would lay them in our hands so we could throw them for him. He always stripped all the fuzz off them before he would play. He also loved plastic bottles, empty or not. He would put his front teeth on a bottle and by moving backwards would roll it everywhere. I had to tie my cabinets shut to keep him from getting plastic bottles out! At bedtime he would go jump up in our bed and put his head on my pillow.

ESPRIT DAVIES
ST. THOMAS, U.S. VIRGIN ISLANDS

sprit is a sweet-natured and bighearted Weimaraner who loves to sunbathe on the warm tile deck surrounding her mountainside home above the Caribbean Sea. In contrast to her adopted Weimaraner sister Gelert, Esprit takes time to smell the hibiscus. And while she barks with Gelert and their adopted terrier cousin Beeper Thompson at the iguanas sunning themselves in the bush, no one thinks Esprit has ever really known what they bark at or why. Esprit, ever faithful, is always at Gelert's side and she loves her family very much. Esprit's favorite book is *Cinderella* by William Wegman.

ETERNAL HOPE BERKMAN
NEW YORK CITY, NEW YORK

Eternal Hope is a two-year-old black-and-tan Beagle/Dachshund mix, found living in an abandoned building with a pack of much larger dogs (whom she must have bossed around plenty). Recently, Hope began training to be a visiting pet, and when she completes the twenty-week course sponsored by the Delta Society and given at the ASPCA, she will be certified to visit patients in hospitals and residents in nursing homes. Because she's a service dog, she is allowed to ride on the subway and bus, which generates a lot of conversation. One person commented that she would surely make anyone's day brighter. That's my Hope.

155

FAGAN LACHMAN
LAGUNA HILLS, CALIFORNIA

Fagan is a seven-year-old Golden Retriever/ Saluki mix with the legs of a colt, an aristocratic face, and a coat the color of whipped butter. A very handsome lad indeed. Friendly and spirited, Fagan has an enormous amount of energy, even for a dog half his age! When he was a young, abandoned pup, he was adopted by Larry, who is a cruelty-free animal behavior trainer. Fagan has appeared in videos and classrooms of all ages with his dad, helping to promote a gentler method of animal training. He is also famous for his Wolf Kisses!

FLASH ("FLASHER") HATTERSLEY
FAYETTEVILLE, NORTH CAROLINA

Flash is six years old, mostly Blue Tick Hound, and weighs close to ninety pounds. I've known Flash all his life, having watched his birth. Firstborn and first to the food, his main interests are playing ball, chasing bird and butterfly shadows, sniffing flowers, and marking his territory. He also plays kissy-face through the fence with his girlfriend Sheena the Rottweiler. Intensely curious, he will watch birds and airplanes fly by. Flash may sound harmless and lovable, but try ringing the doorbell when he's home!

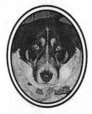

FLASH ROSEANNADANNA SUTHERLAND
MOORELAND, INDIANA

Born July 30, 1981, Flash is a tricolor Basset Hound. She spends most of her time sleeping, begging, and eating. She loves everyone and thinks the world was created solely for her! Her "grandmother" in Illinois said she could visit, but she would have to stay in the basement because no dogs were allowed in her house. Flash spent *one night* in the basement, howling, crying, and moaning. From then on, she was in the house with everyone else, and "Grandma" now cooks breakfast for her (bacon and eggs) while the rest of us eat cereal or rolls!

FLEET-FOOTED FRISBEE
RESTON, VIRGINIA

AKC-registered Fleet-Footed Frisbee is a laid-back, liberated Lhasa Apso with a mind of her own. Her predominantly black hair (speckled with gray as befits her twelve years) is cut short. She begins each day as she has done for the last twelve years: barking at the newspaper boy. Her breakfast routine consists of begging for dog biscuits; with each biscuit, she exits the house by the front door and then returns via the back door to beg for another. Her family agrees that she is the perfect dog, always there, asking for nothing (except biscuits), and enjoying a good stomach scratch daily.

FOSTER (SON OF WHISKERS)
MARTINSBURG, WEST VIRGINIA

Foster is the newest addition to our family and is, by far, the ugliest dog I have ever seen. I generally love all animals, but my parents once adopted a stray dog that resembled the coyote on the Road Runner cartoon. He was not very agreeable and I never liked him very much. I made fun of my parents for having such an ugly dog, which was named Whiskers. Whiskers eventually ran away, but his son was hit on the road in front of my house and I insisted that we take him to the vet. We named him Foster, and now I have the ugliest dog in Martinsburg.

FOZZIE ("FUZZY") SKINNER
JACKSONVILLE, FLORIDA

Weighing in at over ninety pounds, this large Golden Retriever/Belgium Shepherd mix looks much like a pale yellow polar bear. A gentle giant, Fuzzy loves to take a nap. He once napped with a hamburger, complete with bun, in his mouth. (He ate it later when he awakened.) Fuzzy lives on four and a half acres where he enjoys daily "rips" with his father, George Bush Skinner, and baths with his mother, Goldie.

FRANCK OLSON
BELLEVUE, WASHINGTON

Franck, the miniature Dachshund "watchdog" of Trudi Olson, boasts a collection of over forty squeaky toys, one of which is personally chosen each day to be a breakfast or dinner companion (often found floating in the water dish). Franck's engaging personality has netted him many unique gifts from his admirers ... from "Hoover" the barking cookie jar, to an official UW sweatsuit, to mini reindeer antlers. Franck, in full uniform, was featured on local TV's *Parade of Pets* to open the UW Husky football season. His highlight each summer is attending camp "Idle-A-While" with his Mom and Gwamma for "West and Wee-Laxation."

162

FRANÇOIS ("FRENCHY") CORP
SHAWBORO, NORTH CAROLINA

Frenchy is a nine-pound white Toy Poodle with the heart of a lion. He sits on the porch with his chest puffed out surveying his domain. Frenchy loves getting bones at the drive-in window of the bank and can't understand why he doesn't get one at tollbooths and fast-food windows. If he isn't let out of the bedroom in the morning, he will hit the spring-mounted doorstop on the door—*sproing-sproing*—until someone lets him out. He's so excited to see his Aunt Noreen (he used to sleep in her suitcase) that he screams!

FRANÇOIS DIBLEY
TAMPA, FLORIDA

When our precious Poodle, François, was approaching his seventeenth birthday, his mommy Shirley Dibley took pen in hand and François started dictating a friendly greeting to Liberty Ford of 1600 Pennsylvania Avenue. Shortly a letter arrived on White House stationery, along with a picture of the President and Liberty. Five days later we lost our beloved François. Having achieved a degree of notoriety with a biography published by our local newspaper and being mentioned during one of Johnny Carson's monologues ... François' final tribute came when we received personal condolences from President Gerald Ford.

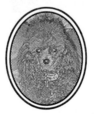

FRANKIE STEINER MEISTER
CHICAGO, ILLINOIS

Frankie Steiner is a very brave boy. He spent most of his terrible twos going back and forth to the vet until we found out he has bad allergies. Now he gets regular allergy shots and he is a trouper about them. These days he is back to chasing squirrels and birds around his yard, playing with all his toys or chewing with his head on a pillow. Frankie likes to spend his days napping or people-watching out the windows. He remains my most, best and always puppy.

FRECKLES TOPO
MILFORD, CONNECTICUT

F reckles is an eleven-year-old brown-and-white female. She is half Terrier and half Beagle. Freckles is very gentle and playful. We have a stuffed bear collection in the corner of our dining room at floor level. Every couple of months, for some unknown reason, Freckles goes into a frenzy starting with three or four rotations around the dining room table at top speed and ending with a diving assault into our bear collection. We haven't figured out what triggers this little quirk, but it's an event not to be missed. Freckles has one serious vice: homemade chocolate-chip cookies.

FRED HILL
CANTON, NORTH CAROLINA

Fred is a Basset Hound of white, black and brown. He is very fun-loving and enjoys giving and receiving affection. His favorite pastime is sleeping. When he's not sleeping, he's hungry. He weighs quite a bit, and if we didn't watch what he eats, he'd be extremely overweight. Fred has this peculiar sideways look that he gives people when they carry on a conversation with him. In the summer, he loves to stretch out in the sunshine with his hind legs crossed. This makes for quite a picture.

FREDA STEVENS
O'FALLON, MISSOURI

When we got Freda at the Humane Society, they said she was a German Shepherd mix, but Freda looks like a hound dog with reddish brown fur. Her claim to fame involves the strange things that she does with her blanket. Freda will go into her room, get her blanket from her kennel, and proceed to drag it into the living room. She'll scratch at the blanket, turn around in circles on it, and then, finally, lie down next to it. Then, while lying spread-eagled, she'll suck on her blanket. Occasionally she'll even fall asleep while in this position. Freda is very weird.

FREDERICK ("FRITZ") VON FACKLAMM
DANIEL, WYOMING

F ritz is a large black-and-tan male German Shepherd. He was diagnosed as having parvus when he was two; lost one eye due to injury at four and the second also due to injury at six. He's now nine, and the combination of his grand courage and his "seeing-eye person" enables him to lead a joyful and complete life. Verbal commands make remote control possible; he memorizes new areas quickly, and enjoys playing with other dogs and his very own cat, Miky. His favorite toys are flexible disks that he catches out of the air or retrieves.

FRENIA FIDO HOTCHKISS
SPRINGFIELD, MICHIGAN

Frenia is a blue Australian Shepherd and a very loving individual. She and I met over thirteen years ago and have been the best of friends ever since. When we first met, she was so cute I just couldn't resist the urge to give her a big hug, and much to my surprise she sounded more like a pig than a puppy. Frenia came home with me that day and we have spent many happy days together. To this day, when I give her a hug, she still squeals like the little pig she tried to pass herself off as that first day!

FREUD ("PUTZ") SCHUSTER
RIALTO, CALIFORNIA

Freud is our California girl. A beautiful Belgian Malinois mix, she came home with us one day as a stray puppy. She never lets her parents fight without barking to break it up, and she goes on every vacation and hiking trip to the mountains, the national parks, or the ocean. She is our "kid" at Christmas (opening her own presents), our marriage counselor, our source of laughter, and we have "family day" with her every weekend. She gives "smoogey-woogeys" on command—that's "gimme kiss."

FRISKY TOWNSEND
SCHENECTADY, NEW YORK

Frisky is no longer with us, but he was our beloved and faithful dog for twenty-one years. He was a mix, Beagle and Terrier. He remained healthy until just before he died and was always at our feet. His vocabulary was wide, but one unusual word worried him. That word was "dictionary," and whenever he heard it, he would run and hide. His folks played Scrabble, often, and when there was a challenge, the word was used—probably in a not so gentle a tone! Frisky decided he simply did not want to get mixed up with that "dictionary"—whatever it was!

FRITZIE DUNCAN
PENSACOLA, FLORIDA

Fritzie is a handsome Terrier, with his mother's sweet disposition and his father's combat genius. This trooper patrols the yard seeking the enemy (birds and squirrels). Intelligence reports invasion by airborne troops: he dispatches them quickly. Now for the advancing legions of squirrels: he's outnumbered, but pushes them beyond the front line and recaptures the hill. Darkness falls, and while lying on his back, feet in the air, snuggled between Mom and Dad, he dreams of new battles.

FROLIC ("MOONBUNNY") JONES
AMAGANSETT, NEW YORK

Frolic is a ten-pound Yorkshire Terrier who has the heart and courage of a lion. Though stricken with a deadly disease (GME) at the age of three, Frolic has defied all the odds and lived eight years—so far! The doctors say she has fought and lived because of the great love that exists between her and her human mom. Frolic loves to play tricks like knocking over trash cans and ripping up all the contents, or eating her mom's diamond earrings. She especially loves eating anything and sleeping under the covers snuggled right next to her mom.

FU TAIE
SPOKANE, WASHINGTON

Battered, bruised, and hungry, he arrived at midnight. Beneath the dirt was twenty-five pounds of white, black-and-brown-spotted, wirehaired dynamite (probably Terrier/Beagle origin), sporting a long, distinctive Fu Manchu mustache. Fond of ice cream and popcorn, Fu would jump and spin about earning his treats as well as his nickname, "The Circus Dog." Charmed by music, he would rock to bebop or swoon to a lullaby, and even taught himself to sing. Not so much a dog as an attitude, full of spit and vinegar, Fu lives on as spirited delight in our lives.

GABBY GLATTLI
DEERFIELD BEACH, FLORIDA

Gabby is a pitch-black Cocker Spaniel with not one hair of another color on her. She was found in a dumpster along with four brothers and sisters. She was so frightened and quiet when we found her, we thought she would never even bark. She became inseparable from me (her mom) and is the sweetest, most loving dog in the world. She meets me at the door when I come home from work with her tiny tail wagging and her dog biscuit in her mouth. She has given me many hours of company and immeasurable love.

GABRIEL JULIAN GREEN-LANGFORD
TACOMA, WASHINGTON

Gabe is a five-year-old Golden Retriever. He is friendly, sensitive, and very intelligent. When he was a puppy, his favorite activity was getting into the bathroom and rolling the toilet paper out—even outdoors, if not caught and stopped. Now he believes he is the father of Panther, a four-year-old black Lab Retriever, and grooms him and growls with him when their territory has been invaded. They love playing together, especially tug-of-war. When a visitor arrives, Gabe will pick up one of his toys and prance around as if he is offering the visitor a great gift.

Gaily Quayle of Walloon Lake ("Quayle Doody")
Walloon Lake, Michigan

Quayle Doody was born in Alexandria, Kentucky. Her most extraordinary accomplishment is that she has never barked for a piece of food, but instead focuses on one's indulgence with sad, starving eyes. Quayle only barks in her role as protector. Her favorite pastimes include eating, jogging, licking, and dreaming of food. She loves to play, but not always in the presence of her brother's overwhelming behavior. Quayle's a bit of a loner, independent, and a good listener. A female to the core, she's extremely intelligent. Quayle means the world to me.

GAST SZABO
CHICAGO, ILLINOIS

Gast is a one-year-old sable German Shepherd who could easily play for a major league baseball club with his love for and skill at playing ball. He likes long walks (sometimes carrying his own leash in his mouth), giving hugs, and playing with his best friend Ripley, a two-year-old Golden Retriever. He enjoys picking apples from the low branches of the tree in the yard. If you sneeze, he never misses a chance to run to your aid and kiss and hug you and make sure you're all right.

GENEVIEVE BEAUTYHEART MACDOUGALL JOHNSON
SALEM, MASSACHUSETTS

Gen is part Elkhound, part Schnauzer, and weighs twenty-six pounds. In the winter, with her full coat, she looks like a baby Husky. In the summer, stripped down, she metamorphoses into a Schnauzer. She has bright root-beer eyes, uses her paws like a cat, and loves to hold your hand. She is very talkative and makes the strangest sounds. She herds you in the direction she wants you to go and loves to watch you cook. She has a sweet disposition but sometimes is too serious, although she's learning to lighten up.

GENGHIS KHAN II ("BUSTER") NORDQUIST
EVERGREEN, COLORADO

Buster was my son's Christmas gift in 1988. With a face you couldn't help but love and a personality that would melt even the coldest heart, he was the warmth, joy, and laughter in our daily lives. Buster supervised every task, whether it was feeding the horses or cleaning out the garage. He loved to ride in the car, even if it was only to the mailbox and back. His heart was as big as all outdoors, and he would protect you from even the smallest shadow. He was more than a companion. He was my *friend*.

GINGER
RYE BROOK, NEW YORK

A sweetheart of a mutt, Ginger was with us until she was eighteen years old. She was brought home from a pet shop at Christmas and always wore a ribbon on her collar. One day we forgot to put her ribbon on. A neighbor said, "Ginger looks very sad." We realized her ribbon was missing. We put on a new ribbon and her eyes lit up again. Our son loved her very much. From a young boy to being a grown businessman, he would call just to talk to Ginger, nicknamed "Hoover" because she did not let a crumb pass her by.

GINGER
WEST COLUMBIA, SOUTH CAROLINA

Ginger adopted us in 1990, when she was about one year old. She can be ladylike or a rough-and-tumble tomboy. Ginger loves to climb mountains—she even danced for a group of strangers atop a mountain in North Carolina. She enjoys playing "dress-up," walking on her back legs, and turning circles. At 23 pounds, Ginger loves to wrestle with our 53-pound Basset Hound, often getting the upper hand. She also likes to play ball. She seldom barks, and she grins when she gets real excited. Ginger is a wonderful little girl!

GINGER THOMASINA DUNFORD
JACKSONVILLE, FLORIDA

Ginger, a mixed Terrier, is about eleven years old. We got her from K&C Kennels, a special home for pets. Ginger prefers taking walks to anything else in life. All we need to do is hum "It's Walking Ginger Time" (to the tune of "It's Howdy Doody Time") and she starts bouncing off the walls. After we give her something special to eat, we ask "Was it good?" and she licks her chops. "Was it real good?"—her tongue goes wild. "Was it really, *really* good?"—she goes bonkers!

GINGER ("MISS MANNERS") INGALA
MT. SINAI, NEW YORK

Ginger, a female Weimaraner, took her first airplane ride at seven weeks of age when Tom brought her home from Florida. She always loved the sunshine and had a neat trick to ensure she wouldn't miss out. While all the dogs were lying on my bed, she would jump off and run barking to the front door. The other dogs would investigate and Ginger would jump back on the bed, making sure she was in the spot where the sun was. She also made a wonderful mother.

GOLDEN CHISMAN, CGC
HAMPTON, VIRGINIA

I don't know what I'd do without you. Who else would bark hysterically to let the neighbors know I've come home in the wee hours of the morning? How else would I find all the socks you retrieve from the middle of the floor? If I threw away a paper product, and it actually stayed gone, I might faint. You are my best friend, my love bug; my big wookie who rolls on the couch, licks my tears when I cry, and chews on the cat "just because." There'll never be another—I hope.

GOLDIE TRIPLETT
LITTLE RIVER, SOUTH CAROLINA

Goldie, a Collie, ran away from her "dog-sitter" while we were relocating to the South. She trekked through ice, snow, and traffic as she tried to find her way home. A wonderful couple found her trying to keep warm and took her to the Animal Shelter, where they checked on her daily. Arriving home, I found a note attached to my garage telling me where to find her. Every year we get a Christmas card, and they have even come to our home for a visit. Truly, a Lassie-come-home story! Goldie is seventeen now and sleeps all day, guards all night.

GRACIE
BROOKLINE, MASSACHUSETTS

G racie was a Lhasa Apso puppy smuggled out of Tibet by an American airman in 1946 when the breed was considered to be sacred and not allowed out. (The Dalai Lama had given one to Lowell Thomas previously.) When Gracie was one year old, the flier's mother gave her to my father, who had admired her. He removed her gray, matted coat, exposing a white coat. She was a conversation piece. At times, to avoid explaining what she was and her background, we said she was a "Poodle"!

GRAF SCHATZ VON DUERR
LITTLE ROCK, ARKANSAS

The nickname Highpoint Hound rang
throughout the fifty states
Forty-two summits he conquered with
his biped mates
For he bore his own backpack like a royal soldier
His success produced a canine world record-
holder
Ultra-runners voted him into club membership
Into oceans and wild rivers he would take a dip
Schatz was the name of the "treasure" or "dear"
A white German Shepherd whose regal lineage
was clear
Succumbed to cancer after a mere ten and one-
half years
His memory lives on in hearts of humans and
peers
We miss you, Schatzeli!

GRAPES BIGLOW
FRESNO, CALIFORNIA

Grapes, a remarkably intelligent and beautiful eighty-seven-pound lapdog with lists of accomplishments too numerous to mention, was born in July 1983 to a German-Australian Shepherd mix mother and a Queensland father and named after her favorite puppy food: the Thompson seedless grapes she ate from the backyard vines. Another favorite food is artichokes, eaten with proper leaf-scraping technique. Grapes bicycles and roller-blades naturally on a leash, which allows for "walks" at proper dog-speed. Grapes won the local PBS "Are You Being Served" contest with her ambiguously risqué entry and enjoys wearing her pearl necklaces, inherited from her late mistress.

190

GULLIVER EDEN
NEW YORK, NEW YORK

Named after the fictional character who traveled to a strange new world, Gulliver was born in Fredericia, Denmark, and traveled to New York when he was four months old. The transition to American life was easy since he had been listening to English tapes since brith. An operatic tenor, he particularly enjoys singing duets with Dame Joan Sutherland and Kiri Tekanawa. The Bell Duet from *Lakmé* becomes a trio when Gulliver starts to sing. An adaptable traveler, Gulliver sofa-hops between New York City, Southampton, and upstate New York. Incidentally, Gulliver is a black Royal Standard Poodle, whose parents are international champions.

GUS ("GUSBABY") EPPES
HOUSTON, TEXAS

G us, a Terrier X, was born approximately May 1, 1986, and weighs twenty-two pounds. He looks a lot like Benji and wears a toddler 4 T-shirt. He has a couple of bad habits. He bites frogs and chases all cats out of his backyard. He also gets under the dining table, pushes a chair out, then hops in the chair and onto the table so that he can see if his "mommy" is home. He would rather have a hug than food—unless it's his favorite food, a Whataburger!

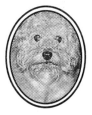

HADLEY KOSS
NEW YORK, NEW YORK

Hadley, a sixteen-pound wheat-colored Pekingese, was born May 17, 1989. He loves apples, carrots, and any other food you may feed him, which explains his girth! Hadley is famous for his almost toothless grin and his ability to sit up and walk backwards on his hind legs. His favorite activity is sleeping with his head propped up against the wall. He is often mistaken for a girl since he has such a beautiful, fluffy coat, but he is really a macho man!

HAMLET BARTOLETT KLINE
MARGATE, NEW JERSEY

Hamlet (L'Enchanteur Noir de Michelle) is a six-year-old black Miniature Poodle. He is extremely friendly and intelligent. Some of the tricks he has taught himself are how to open peanuts, how to open doors, and how to sneak candy out of closed boxes. He loves to play with his toys and humors us by allowing us, reluctantly, to dress him up. Never does he want to leave us, and he especially enjoys going with us on sailboats, windsurfers, motorcycles, bicycles, waverunners, and snow skis.

HEIDI NIELSON
EMERYVILLE, CALIFORNIA

Many people think Heidi is a Belgian Shepherd needing a diet, but she's actually a Collie/Black Labrador Retriever cross with a very thick double coat. Heidi and her sister, Sydney, were born August 8, 1982. Heidi is our "people dog," who does one of the best "No one's petted me since 1953" routines ever seen. She has patiently introduced countless children to the joy of petting a nice dog (sometimes they get kisses, too). Heidi likes to chase squirrels, and doesn't swim but wades or sits in the water when we go to the dog park. She made "angels in the snow" when we were in Boston for two winters.

HEIDI ROSS
SIMI, CALIFORNIA

Heidi was found amongst bags of garbage in a bad area of Los Angeles. Her expressive eyes were pleading for help when she was spotted by a passing woman who scooped her up. Her rescuer, Max Andrews, found her a loving home with a wonderful family. She now lives in a beautiful, big house with three boys she loves to play soccer with. A true rags-to-riches story, Heidi is the constant and faithful companion of her mom, Cristy.

HENRI "THE GERMAN LEANERSNEAKER"
RICHMOND, VIRGINIA

Henri was a low, slow, toe tappin', sneaking for toilet water, hundred pount, hunk of love. This dog had soul and sang the blues to every passing siren. Loved to retrieve frisbees, balls, sticks, snowballs or any object I would throw. During hot humid summers, I'd find him sleeping in the tub to cool down. Always ready to play, work, eat, sleep or lean against you for scratches and lovin'. He would talk with his eyes. If I felt bad he took care of me. He loved Cookie the Great Dane. I loved him.

HENRY WADSWORTH BERKMAN
NEW YORK, NEW YORK

Henry Wadsworth is an eight-year-old red longhaired Substandard (which has nothing to do with his mentality) Dachshund. He is, as his name implies, a very long fellow. He also has pudgy paws that flip-flop on the floor like oversize galoshes when he walks through his house. Henry loves to go on vanity walks but prefers to ride in his patchwork shoulder tote, where he hunkers down with only his long nose pointing skyward. He also loves to motor; once he just hopped into an open taxicab along with a very startled passenger.

HOMER WITTFELT
LONGMONT, COLORADO

Homer is a retired racing Greyhound, a ninety-two-pound fawn-and-white baby, born in March 1990. His name fits! Homer is a laid-back clown who loves flowers. He's my PR guy for Greyhounds As Pets. His favorite toy is a stuffed bunny. Homer enjoys tea parties with our two-year-old granddaughter. He is the essence of patience. He watches wildlife specials on TV and can't quite figure out how all those animals are in that box! Homer shares our home with four other dogs and three cats.

H.R.H. SUSHI-SAN KINSEY
PACIFIC PALISADES, CALIFORNIA

H.R.H. is an important member of an international group of artists and collectors of a rare Japanese art form called Netsuke, the most sophisticated form of small sculpture. She has the vital function of being a patroness and pivotal link of communication with this group. Her associates include royalty, heads of state, and the diplomatic corps of powerful nations. She also has a magnificent collection of jewelry and unique gifts received from her loyal friends throughout this global community. She's a gracious hostess and adored by all her subjects.

200

HOUDINI
EL PASO, TEXAS

Houdini was rescued from the Animal Shelter on February 2, 1993, after my pet of ten years died. He is now eleven months old. He is a purebred German Shepherd, almost all black with tan paws, very playful but as tricky as his name implies. Incredibly smart and rebellious, he watches everything I do and then reverses it in less time than it took me to do it to begin with. He has managed to break several thick chains and has pried open the links of bigger chains to set himself free. I don't believe in reincarnation, but . . .

HUEY BROVILLETTE
FORESTDALE, MASSACHUSETTS

Huey is a lifesaver! He's been my guide dog for four months and we really work together as a team. Twice, when crossing the street, Huey has stepped in front of me, blocking my path and preventing me from being hit by a car. During a hospitalization, I became unconscious and Huey ran to get the nurse. Huey is a gentle, loving, hardworking yellow Lab who's always there for me. When not working, he loves to play ball or tug-of-war. He takes care of me and I spoil him. This summer I think I'll teach him to swim!

HUMPHREY HOROWITZ (SIR HUMPHREY HO)
WESTFIELD, NEW JERSEY

Our Shar Pei, Humphrey, has a wonderful disposition. Lovable and sweet, "H" weighs sixty-seven pounds and is mostly muscle, except for his fat, wrinkly face. Physically, Humphrey appears threatening, but fearless he's not—just ask the realtors. He also yelps like a Poodle to get his way. Humphrey enjoys gin cubes, hide-and-seek, watching squirrels, and hooching. Notable incidents: twelve miles solo, skunk attack, wet-paint paws, fried fish/tartar sauce, food bag attack, three pounds of cream cheese, and "Unleash me, I won't run away; I promise." Never a dull moment and never a dog as loved as he! Humphrey is King!

HUMPHREY LIEBERMAN
PLANTATION, FLORIDA

Humphrey is a spunky, fourteen-year-old, formerly all-black Chihuahua. As he begins to sport more white hair than black, his energy has not decreased one iota. He is still very much in (unrequited) love with Casablanca, his companion of eleven years. Humphrey makes a lasting impression with all who meet him—not always a good impression, but definitely unforgettable. Our favorite trait of Humphrey's is his absolute lack of the concept of time. Whether we are gone for five seconds or five weeks, we get the same shriek of delight when we return.

INKY SEWALK
TEANECK, NEW JERSEY

Inky is a young lady who prefers not to give her age. Charcoal-black and cunning in curls, she simply can't keep her ears out of anything. This spunky little Cocker Spaniel thinks vanilla ice cream is the cat's meow. A proper lady, she spends most evenings at home—listening to classical music or languishing in the bath. When she's in full swing, you might find her at the driving range, chewing on the Oriental, or trying to convince Kate that maybe the third floor would be a great Inky-pad.

IRISH WELCH
TUCSON, ARIZONA

I rish, named because of his reddish hair, is a five-year-old Miniature Poodle. Even though he lives in the desert, he is a connoisseur of dog sweaters and refuses to sleep without one in the winter months. An excellent swimmer and diver, Irish's longest dive has been recorded at eight feet. His favorite trick is to get a dog biscuit, run away with it, and tease his best friend Shauna, a black Standard Poodle, until she comes chasing after him. He loves to have his photo taken anytime and to go for a ride in the car anytime. He's a lover!

IVYROSES' MILADY APPLEGARTH ("ZOE")
HANNASTOWN, PENNSYLVANIA

*Z*oe is an eighteen-month-old registered Border Collie. She is black, white, and tan, weighs thirty-eight pounds, and is twenty inches tall. Her favorite activities are sheepherding, obedience, frisbee, playing ball, and more sheepherding. Zoe is a very intense young lady who tends to take life a little too seriously. She does have a fun side because she likes to sleep on the couch when nobody is looking. Her nickname is Peanut because she is smaller than the rest of the clan. Zoe owns and loves Jan and Bob.

IZABO DEPRIEST-CHALMERS
LANSING, MICHIGAN

I zabo DePriest-Chalmers was born September 26, 1987, to a purebred Springer Spaniel and her wandering lover. Her black and white markings, her curly-haired ears, and the "Free Puppies" sign proved too much to resist—she entered her new family's new home in Lansing. She showers everyone who enters with affection. Once she lays her head on your knee and looks up at you with her big brown eyes, you're hooked. She loves to look out the living room window, stand guard in the front yard, have her belly rubbed, and lean against anyone who will give her attention.

JACKIE BLACK BEAR SULLIVAN
NEWARK, OHIO

J ackie is a purebred black Pomeranian puppy. She has white spots. They are on her chin, her two back legs near her tail, the tips of her feet, and between her front legs. She loves to bark at the donkeys and cows behind her mistress's house. One of her other "hobbies" is to step on her squeaky toy, bark, put her ears back, then race around the house, stop, jump onto the couch, bark, and jump down. She does this over and over. She also likes to follow her mistress around the house.

JAKE THE BEAR
FRANKTOWN, COLORADO

Jake was an Irish Wolfhound who thought he was a lap dog. His favorite spot was the davenport, relegating everyone else to the floor. He and his half-sister, Morgan, enjoyed "singing" together, both in the house and outside, throwing their heads back and howling. He was also a great watchdog (never barked but had a tremendous growl). One night he scared us all out of bed with a huge growl. An errant helium balloon was floating at head level in the bedroom doorway and we all thought we had a prowler. Poor Jake was terrified of balloons after that.

JAMIE MIZUFUKA
HAWTHORNE, CALIFORNIA

In loving memory of Jamie (August 1977– Feburary 1992). He was a Yorkshire Terrier with black and tan markings. Jamie weighed six pounds. He loved Liv-A-Snaps treats and would try to bury them under any rug. He liked to be scratched behind the ears and would constantly push at your hand to have this done. Jamie's favorite sport was stealing socks and hiding them in the house! But Jamie was really animated when the telephone rang . . . he would just sit there and howl until someone answered it!

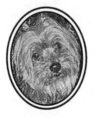

JASON MONTGOMERY
WILMINGTON, DELAWARE

J ason is a ten-year-old Golden Retriever, born March 1, 1982. He loves going for a daily walk and eating delicious treats like chicken livers and ice cream. He lives up to his breed's special talent for retrieving things, especially ladies' purses and men's baseball caps. Jason also enjoys playing with his brother Taylor, a Golden Retriever. He likes taking care of him and they are best buddies. Jason is a good-natured and lovable "pup boy"!

JASPER ("JAZZ") KELLY
NASHVILLE, TENNESSEE

Born November 18, 1985, in Nashville, Tennessee, Jazz is a Siberian Husky/German Shepherd mix with the most splendid personality. Jazz has no idea he is of the canine persuasion, which makes him incredibly fun to be around. He loves to go for walks and rides in the car. After a hard day of snoozing, it's wonderful to stretch out in Dad's recliner (with Dad in it, of course!) or, if he's bounding with energy, to bring us every rubber toy he owns. More than anything, Jazz brings us incalculable joy and happiness, while teaching us the meaning of love, daily.

JEAN-LUK ANTHONY
HOUSTON, TEXAS

Jean-Luk is the champion underwear stealer of all time. It is common to be talking on the phone and see a piece of your underwear go by into the kitchen. A four-pound Pomeranian, Jean-Luk has the "spectacles" of a Keeshond, so with his black muzzle and "glasses" his face is always very expressive. His questioning looks, as if he just can't understand what you're saying, can make anyone chuckle. He enjoys his wrestling matches with his dad and likes to chase his cat friend Leon.

JEAN QUINCY LaFEET
SALISBURY, NORTH CAROLINA

I n a flash of black with ears streaming behind him, Jean Quincy LaFeet retrieves his ball. Liquid brown eyes gleaming with intelligence, he flattens his belly to the ground in anticipation of another throw. Like his buccaneer namesake, Jean LaFeet is an intrepid creature with both brains and stylish looks. He is the Perfect Poodle. His tastes are simple—he desires only the best. He has given us nothing but joy! If Quincy could speak, we know that he would have a good vocabulary and be highly articulate. We do not consider him a dog, and neither does he.

JENNY ("WOLF") SAVITT
NORTH SALEM, NEW YORK

Jenny, a fifteen-year-old Norwegian Elkhound, owes her longevity to a lethargic lifestyle, punctuated by the occasional mad dash to the dinner bowl. Hers is a prodigious appetite guided by a simple maxim: if it can be chewed, it must be edible. Seldom one for a wild romp in the woods, Jenny prefers to experience life lying on her side, shedding truckloads of Elkhound fur. Though ready to woof at any suspicious sound, she's generally indifferent to man and beast alike, and her temperament is always a sweet one.

JESSE DRAGONE
LONG ISLAND, NEW YORK

Jesse is a five year old black Lab, adopted from North Shore Animal League on August 22, 1989. He's gentle, affectionate and very playful. When he wants to play fetch, he will bring his toys to you, one by one, until you play with him. His favorite things: finding treats that his pal Scrappy hides, waiting everyday by the window for the mailman and chasing birds and squirrels.

JESSE JAMES DOAK
NEW CUMBERLAND, WEST VIRGINIA

Jesse is a seven-year-old, black-and-white All-American dog who loves taking walks when I ride my horse, Garwild. He had an infection when he was little and now has vision in only one eye. Jesse caused some panic recently by disappearing for eighteen hours when he walked home nearly twenty miles after deciding he didn't like the place he was visiting. He arrived safe and sound, and got his picture in the local paper. These days the celebrity dog enjoys relaxing in the sun and playing with his friends.

JINNY MALKIN
TENAFLY, NEW JERSEY

Jinny, a Golden Retriever, was a member of our family for fourteen years. She was well loved by us and loved us each in return, but she especially loved our mom. When Mom was homebound by a broken leg, a local organization brought her lunch daily. The delivery man was afraid of dogs and wouldn't come to the door, but instead placed the food in the driveway. After he left each day, Mom opened the door and Jinny trotted out. She proudly carried in *first* the milk carton and *then* the food container, never trying to steal a taste for herself.

J.J. JACKMAN
WALLINGFORD, CONNECTICUT

J.J., a Sheltie, just celebrated his fourth birthday. His favorite activity is a roughhouse session with Daddy. His biggest goal in life is to see how fast he can zoom through the house without breaking the sound barrier. He protects his older brother Baron and they spend a hundred percent of their waking hours together, mostly playing and protecting their property. J.J. loves party hats, having his picture taken, putting on his bow tie, and assuming the role of host and official greeter for our dinner guests. He also provides the entertainment, singing requests.

JOEY ("BAD BOY") GARLAND
GREEN COVE SPRINGS, FLORIDA

Joey is a Heinz 57 variety with lots of auburn hair and bright, beautiful brown eyes. He's sweet, funny, and the "spokesdog" for the rest of the dogs in the yard. Joey thinks he's a goat, so we must keep all paper, rags, etc., out of his reach. He loves to put empty garden pots over his head and run blindly through the yard. He rants and raves to himself and likes to roll on his back on top of balls and pinecones. He's a flea bag and has no teeth—but we love him!

JONES, BISHOP
AMAGANSETT, NEW YORK

Bishop is a Bearded Collie whose biggest ambition in life is to actually catch a sea gull. She obsessively delights in patrolling the beach at warp speed but never quite seems to get the prize. While waiting for her prey to appear, she is delighted to go for a swim or stage an air-sea battle with her best friend, Kiri. Bishop is also the best alarm clock a person could have. Every morning, at 6 A.M. sharp, she leaps from the end of the bed, flies through the air and lands on my head. You may think "Lucky Me." You would be right. She's the greatest!

JOSH SPARROWOODS TAYLOR TUCKER
HICKORY, NORTH CAROLINA

Taylor is snow-white with black expressive eyes and a black nose. He's a seven-year-old West Highland Terrier. Taylor demands and will get attention if he has to slap you with his paw or bring his toy and drop it in your lap. Sorry, Vanna, but he doesn't like *Wheel of Fortune*; every time it comes on and a new puzzle comes up, he barks and leaves the room. Most dogs protect you from intruders, but not Taylor—he protects us from bees and flies. Once you own a Westie, you're hooked.

J.R. TRENNER
LAS VEGAS, NEVADA

J.R. is very protective of his humans and his truck. He travels extensively around the United States, helping us to make it safe and sound to horse shows. He has both human and animal friends nationwide. J.R. has appeared on network TV, opening the show *Prime Time Pets* on CBS. He rode the hotwalker (hanging by his teeth from the rope) and did one of his best dives into the horse trough. Everyone agreed he was the star of the show. Being a Queensland Heeler, he is very photogenic, athletic, and highly intelligent. He is the finest dog person there is.

K-9 SAM
HIGH POINT, NORTH CAROLINA

K-9 Sam, a purebred Belgian Malinois, was purchased by the High Point Police Department in November 1990, and his career as a police canine began. He is handled by Officer Daryl Delagrange. Sam is the son of Kastor, who retired from the Greensboro Police Department and was recognized as one of the most famous police dogs of all time. During his career, Sam has demonstrated the working ability, intelligence, and courage synonymous with his breed, and he is credited with numerous felony and misdemeanor arrests. Sam proudly serves his community—and the spirit of Kastor lives on!

KAI'S "KITO" OF ROCKING HI
MCCOOK, NEBRASKA

November 9, 1980 – February 19, 1992. Kito was a handsome Keeshond, and his outstanding performances in the show and obedience ring were not nearly as important as his companionship. He was a gentle and trusting friend.

KALOLIE'S GRAYEREST BONNIE ELEGANCE GERTY
GARDINER, NEW YORK

Bonnie arrived early in 1993 and quickly established herself as the overseer of the family domain. She watches with alert eyes and challenges family and visitors with a soft bark, then she shakes, wiggles, and wags to greet them, and finally runs over and nuzzles her new friends. As befits her name, she sits and trots with golden elegance, a tawny figure on the green lawn or a blur of amber against the trees. She will grow and mature into the stately Collie she is.

KATEY MAREE LOVE
BAKERSFIELD, CALIFORNIA

Katey is a gorgeous Norwegian Elkhound. Her tail curls up even tighter than normal when she gets happy or excited, and the coloring and shape of her eyebrows make her look perpetually worried. Although she believes she's still a puppy and therefore a lapdog, Katey is almost three years old. When she wants to give you kisses, she'll plop her paws on your arm or legs as if you're her prey. Even though she sounds as fierce as a bear while playing and is over twice their size, she'll cry when one of the other dogs is playing with her toys.

KATIANNA KUERZI
MIDWAY CITY, CALIFORNIA

Katianna or Kat or Rammer is a nine-year-old brindle American Pit Bull Terrier. She is a wonderful result of the Animal Control adoption program. She was a year old when we brought her home to guard our yard. She is a typical Pit Bull—loving and cheerful—and only functions as a guard because of her size and form. This calm, happy animal rams her way into the life of every human she meets. Her favorite activity is sitting on the top of her doghouse, surveying the world and waiting patiently for someone to lick.

KATIE CALL
SALT ROCK, WEST VIRGINIA

Katie, our three-year-old chocolate Cocker Spaniel, has more spirit and determination than anyone I know. She's been blind half her life due to genetic causes, but she doesn't let that slow her down! She likes to go for walks in the fields, and if she bumps into something, she just changes course a little. She loves to steal (and eat) green peppers from the garden and thinks the backyard fish pond is her personal water dish. Saturday mornings are for lying on Dad's lap in the recliner. We feel God blessed us by sending Katie into our lives.

KATIE MAE ELISAR
COLUMBUS, OHIO

K atie, named for the Grateful Dead tune "Katie Mae," is a four-year-old yellow Lab who was adopted from a kennel just before she turned two. Initially very shy and reserved, Katie has slowly come out of her shell to become a happy, loving dog who enjoys long car rides, power walks, and giving her affectionate "typewriter teeth" bites. Her favorite friends include neighborhood friend Fletch and long-distance cousin Baxter. As she (occasionally) works to regain her hour/glass figure, her greatest nemesis is dog biscuits and Grandma Bette's homemade cheese bread.

KATIE ZOSCHAK
NORTH GROSVENORDALE, CONNECTICUT

Katie is a three-year-old, somewhat over-weight Cocker Spaniel. Her favorite pastime is eating. She shares her kennel and house with two male Labs and one female Shepherd. She has been known to hang on to her brother Flash's lip and chase him around when things don't go her way. Although she appears to be brave, she hides out during thunderstorms. Her snooty and bratty personality has caused her to be referred to as Katie Simpson, a relative of Bart. She dislikes all strangers, especially women, and must *always* have her own way.

KILLER RETTIG
ALPHARETTA, GEORGIA

Killer has worked as a blood donor and guard dog at Atlanta Animal Hospital for fourteen years. A 120-pound Rottweiler, Killer will herd any after-hours intruder into a corner until someone responds to her barking. She has thwarted four burglary attempts and one robbery. Killer enjoys demonstrating obedience, guard, and seeing-eye training to many local schools. She is trained to herd escaped pets back into the hospital, and has done so for dogs, cats, birds, sheep, and monkeys. She is also trained to jump between any aggressive animal and a staff member, but never to hurt another animal under any condition. What would we do without Killer?

KING ("BUSTER") NAPOLEON
DERBY, CONNECTICUT

orn on the Fourth of July, he was never the mild-mannered Malamute we thought he would be. With his surprising size and his unquenchable thirst for getting into trouble, he certainly has become a true "Buster." New York City streets come in second compared to our yard—Buster's digging ability is better than most backhoes. But even with a battle-scarred yard and broken tree limbs scattered throughout, he's a great companion and friend. Kids love Buster, and Buster loves kids. He thinks he's one of them. Everybody knows Buster.

KOKOMO CHIEN DAE TAS
WISE, VIRGINIA

Kokomo is a black Teacup Poodle. His nickname is Toe. He is one and a half years old. For such a little bundle of joy, Kokomo has the attitude of an American Pit Bull Terrier. He hasn't realized he only weighs three pounds. His favorite pastime is guarding little pieces of food (while showing his tiny white fangs) from anything and everything, even from our 110-pound Rottweiler named Tori. Kokomo's need for love is never ending. He has to have total attention one hundred percent of the time. As ruler of the household, he brings nothing but smiles to everyone he encounters.

LADDIE HARVEY
EL SEGUNDO, CALIFORNIA

L addie is a beautiful Sheltie and my best friend. He will be twenty years young on June 7, 1993. He sleeps a lot these days, but in April, out of 100-plus entries in Sun City's Pet Parade, he won a First Place Blue Ribbon for Liveliest and Noisiest Pet. His walks are shorter now, but he still greets everyone he meets. He likes to play with his toys if I join in. Laddie has comforted me through life's trials and tribulations and shared my happy moments, too. His vet calls him a miracle dog, and so do I!

236

LADY
CERES, CALIFORINA

When our son, Ross, was two years old, we bought him a Newfoundland puppy. Lady followed Ross everywhere he went. One day while I was milking in the goat barn the neighbor heard Lady frantically barking and found her watching Ross, who was looking into a muddy pool of water under the canal bridge. Another day she pawed my husband until he went with her down to the high stack of baled hay in the barn, where Ross had climbed up to the top and was peering down at the cement floor. When Ross began playing in the water troughs, Lady barked to notify us.

LADY BENTLEY ("LIBBY") BRACEWELL IANDOLI
WEST NEWTON, MASSACHUSETTS

Libby is a four-year-old, three-pound, bow-legged Yorkie who's convinced she's a Great Dane. Because Libby is so small, she's also called "Rodentsky" or "Tiny." Libby was an anniversary present, named after two restaurants in London, England. She has an older brother, Benson and sister, Coco. The "Kids" are the proud owners of a Range Rover with the license plate "Yorkie." They have a big birthday party in October with friends, presents, cake and Bailey's Irish Cream. Libby loves playing with Snoopy's, a toy hamburger and her big sister Coco. She also likes riding in Mom's mini-Cooper and swimming in the pool.

LADY COCO KHANEL IANDOLI
WEST NEWTON, MASSACHUSETTS

Coco is a six-year-old, eight-pound Yorkie who loves to cuddle and thinks she's a delicate princess. She enjoys being groomed, wearing bows and pearls, dancing with Daddy, and her favorite exercise is eating (especially grapes). Daddy calls her "Moose" because she's such a big Yorkie. Coco ("Beautiful" or "Cocalina") was a Christmas puppy, named after the designer Coco Chanel. Unlike most Yorkies, her left ear droops and the right one stands up. Coco's favorite toy is her little sister, Libby and she has a big brother, Benson. Coco has the best manners and likes car shows and going swimming with Mommy.

LADY COLELLA
PHILADELPHIA, PENNSYLVANIA

Lady was an English Setter born in 1966 and rescued from the shelter that year. Lady was loving and a homebody. She was content lying with her mistress, or resting under the tree after gardening with her master. She rallied each evening for her nightly run and security check of the large fenced yard, where on many occasions she tangled with opossum. She always managed to snitch food without being seen but was never an overindulger, so the family never knew where they would find a hidden bone or even a blueberry muffin! She has been dearly missed since 1981.

LADY FANCI PANTS BUECHE
HOUSTON, TEXAS

F anci, my sixteen-year-old Yorkshire Terrier, is now a petite fifteen pounds of love who has to be lifted on and off the bed like royalty. Since she's been spoiled all her life with chicken breasts as her main staple, she treats dry dog food as something to bury around *her* house! The TV is on twenty-four hours a day just for her. She has a permanent lipstick stain on her white head where she is kissed every morning before I leave for work (and she begins a tough day of TV and napping). No one could ever be more loved!

LADY KESWICK
RYE BROOK, NEW YORK

Kezzie was a real lady, a beautiful Yorkshire Terrier. When she showed, she just glowed, always turning heads. One day a limo stopped and a chauffeur got out just to pet her. We spoke awhile, then he opened the back door of the limo and there sat a Yorkie, alone on the huge back seat, another beauty.

LADY LOVE MIMI WILLIAMS
JACKSON, MISSISSIPPI

Born October 21, 1989, Lady Love became an instant traveler and pen pal to fifth graders in Louisville, Kentucky, and Oxford, Mississippi. As soon as she sees us packing the motor home, she hits the road running for the door and ready to go. The fifth-graders study all the states and mark off on the map the postcards from Lady Love in her travels. An eighty-two-pound Golden Retriever, Lady Love is the hit of the party when we visit the schoolchildren. Her best friend is Kitty, a white cat who is a fellow traveler and follows us on our walks around the neighborhood.

LADY MAXIE OF FOXLEY
TAMPA, FLORIDA

Maxie is a Border Terrier, one of the rarest breeds in North America. She lives on Sherwood Forest Drive with her loyal friends Kathy Feeney and R.J. Kwap. Maxie weighs sixteen pounds and has a white chest, beautiful brown eyes, and a loving personality. A true Border Terrier, she loves to hunt fox (cats) and rabbits. But her only weapon is her licking tongue—Maxie loves all creatures, great and small. Her favorite treat is beef jerky. Her favorite "boyfriend" is Roy Vance. Her hobbies are chasing balls and meeting people.

LANCELOT THADDEUS QUILTY
FAIRFAX, VIRGINIA

Lance was adopted when he was thirteen months old because he did not measure up to his former owner's Irish Setter. Weighing in at 110 pounds, he is a handsome dog with a thick red overcoat. His birthday is July 2, 1985. We call him Lance Prance because when he walks he resembles a Clydesdale horse with the taffy-colored fur growing between his toes and the way he picks up each front paw and places it just so. He has been visiting nursing homes as a member of the Fairfax Pets on Wheels pet therapy team since 1987.

LANEY'S LITTLE MISS ("MISTY") SHIRDEN
BLANCHESTER, OHIO

Misty is a one-and-a-half-year-old, salt-and-pepper Schnauzer—but we think she must be part rooster and part mountain goat. She almost crows instead of barks and she jumps around like a goat! She enjoys riding in the car and has already taken a vacation in Florida, where she loved the beach. She's very friendly, and like Will Rogers she's never met a person (or animal) she didn't like.

LAUREL BUTLER MACLEAN
CLINTON, MARYLAND

Laurel (nicknamed Rue-Rue because of the noises she makes around dinnertime) is a five-year-old Vizsla. She's been described as a simple dog in a plain brown wrapper. Laurel lived with six other dogs until recently being adopted. With her transition to single life, she is now a certified spoiled brat! She enjoys floating around the pool on her raft, visiting nursing homes, lying on her sack watching TV, and hogging the bed at night. This "laid-back" attitude is complemented by her athletic build and exceptional training as a show dog—a precious, perfect package!

LEXUS ("BUBBA") JOSEPHSON
LAS VEGAS, NEVADA

Born June 15, 1991, at Rolling Gait's Pheasant Run Farm, New York, our precious son Lexus is the most laid-back, docile male Old English Sheepdog and the spitting image of his daddy, John-John, a champion show dog. His granddaddy was a seven-time Grand Champion. He snores louder than the loudest of men. He's also inseparable from his constant companion, Mercedes, and follows her every move. He spends time playing and diving in the pool with Mercedes and his mistress, Sandy. He also loves to ride in the family van in his own captain's chair.

LIBERTY ROPOLO
ITALIAN ALPS, MONTE DELLA LUNA, ITALY

L iberty is a black-and-white English Setter who loves to bird-hunt with her sister, Marshmallow. She feels equally at home in the woods of Italy or Maine. When in Italy, she enjoys sipping cups of unattended coffee, snitching the baby's food, and scouting for unprotected provisions belonging to Alpine skiers. Liberty smiles on command and has a knack for finding laps of friendly guests. As puppies, Liberty and Marshmallow attracted crowds of busy New Yorkers when they instinctively pointed at pigeons in mid-Manhattan.

LIEBCHEN SHIRMER
NEW BRAUNFELS, TEXAS

Liebchen defends the property of Marilyn Shirmer and Uncle Luther from all neighborhood cats. She's a twenty-two-pound Schnauzer with a powerful voicebox, and if you touch Mama's truck you may be torn limb from limb—in the sequence listed in your warning! With family, she is a loving companion and understands any conversation involving Liebchen! She can "read" family car sounds a block away. Her day is spent with Uncle Marvin—big, shady yard, friendly neighbors, car work, beef jerky, and trips to town. When she talks, he always understands the "Go" part!

LIL PEPE OF CREST
DEFUNIAK SPRINGS, FLORIDA

Pepe is a little red Pomeranian dog. He's ten years of age with numerous children, grandchildren, and great-grandchildren, most of which are show dogs. He likes to visit the kennel and enjoys his offspring. He washes their faces and ears, and has a tendency to step back to look and see if he's missed a spot. He had congestive heart failure three years ago, yet he's very active and loving and devoted to his whole family. He sleeps with his mom and dad every night and brings much joy to their lives. He's loved so very much.

LILLY VAN DUSEN
CORAL GABLES, FLORIDA

Lilly Van Dusen is a purebred Wheaten Terrier and the pride and joy of her mother, Susan. Like her sister Celia, she likes to sleep behind the chairs in the sitting room and go "out." She also loves to come in and get her "treat." Lilly is quite the lady—exceptionally well behaved and almost always well groomed (she goes to the beauty parlor quite frequently). Lilly hardly ever suffers from doggy breath despite her slight dental irregularity.

LINDA CHAMIZO
MIAMI, FLORIDA

L inda is a seven-year-old canine angel on earth, a possible German Shepherd/ Golden Retriever mix. Although she thinks she plays second fiddle to her feisty sister, a Schnauzer named Belle, she's really her master's secret love. On April 8, 1985, when she was about nine months old, her master rescued her from spending her life tied to a tree with little water and occasional food. They ran away together to a new home full of all the love this marvelous companion needed and deserved. Loved by all who meet her, she's a real beauty and a spoonful of honey!

LITTLE LORD OLIVER
PITTSBURGH, PENNSYLVANIA

Little Lord Oliver is a Cavalier King Charles Spaniel. An English aristocrat born in Missouri, he moved north and acquired his title at the age of three months, thus becoming Master of Country Club Acres. This position is very important, and he collects homage in the form of waves from passing tenants. Oliver's pastimes include practicing his vocal exercises, watching squirrels, and attending charity events. He employs a houseman, Ben, solely to maintain his bone and ball collections. He is also a noted connoisseur of rawhide and leather goods. Little Lord Oliver is son of the Duke of Yorkshire.

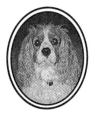

LITTLE RUSTI
BURBANK, CALIFORNIA

Terrified and heartbroken, Little Rusti was rescued from an animal shelter. A ten-year-old cafe au lait Toy Poodle, his time was up when he was adopted on May 11, 1992. Within a short time and with a good diet, Little Rusti had a new lease on life. With his bright, black eyes, heart-shaped nose and crooked smile, he is his mother's constant companion. An affectionate and loving little dog, Little Rusti brings joy and happiness to his parents Max and David.

LOKI HAAG
SOUTH BURLINGTON, VERMONT

Loki is a handsome six-and-a-half-year-old brown Lab. His athletic prowess—especially with a frisbee—is known and admired in three states. Every muscle tensed, he poses ready for each throw and then flies gracefully fifty to seventy-five yards to make his catch. His record is twenty catches in succession. At the lake, he launches himself in a swan dive off a high dock and then swims to retrieve the disk. He is a beautiful sight to behold. At night, he snuggles in his parents' bed and dreams of new athletic challenges while, as always, being the protector "on duty."

LORD BOGART ROEDER
KINGSLAND, GEORGIA

Bogie is an AKC fawn Great Dane. He is not only a gentle giant at almost 200 pounds, but also a great companion and guard dog. He spends most of his time protecting our home, but thinks he owns the neighbors' yards as well—and insists on telling others to move on. His favorite pastimes are racing bicyclists up and down the length of the fence, helping to take the trash out, being the judge for a game of badminton, playing football, and running around the house with a boot in his mouth.

LORD THEODORE
NEW ROCHELLE, NEW YORK

Teddy, a Collie, loved all people and animals. He taught our first child to walk. He would push his hip by her and allow her to hang on to his fur and guide her. A baby-sitter and nanny, he sat in the playpen and watched over her with loving care. He loved the Good Humor man and ran to the door when he heard the bells; he would sit with the baby on the curb, and they would eat the Vanilla Dixies together. He loved walks with his pals Lucky the rabbit and Sam the cat. He cannot be replaced, ever.

LUCKY REISCHE
EUSTIS, FLORIDA

L ucky's age isn't certain, but is around eight to ten years. She is mostly Poodle and Schnauzer, which makes her a Schnoodle! Her favorite pastime is barking. Her favorite sport is barking. She barks at cars, people, lizards, and toads. This is getting better, since she used to bark at doors!

LUCY MARIE MOORMAN
EL PASO, TEXAS

Lucy Marie is a miniature red Dachshund. She had a playpen when she was six weeks old and had to stay in it so she wouldn't get stepped on by Patricia, her adopted mother. She was held and loved more than she stayed in the playpen. After chewing her way out of the pen, she has since learned to sit up, roll over, and play dead if we promise her a snack. She has learned to water-floss her teeth after snacks by holding her mouth over the pop-up water sprinkler heads in her backyard.

LUPO BRANCACCIO
NEW YORK, NEW YORK

Lupo is as pure a Siberian Husky as a dog could be. He is a strong sled dog, active, intelligent, independent, and fast, and possesses great endurance. He is also hardheaded, stubborn, and constantly fighting for dominance. Everything a good Husky should be. Most important, he is my friend and is always there when I need him. Lupo is always happy to practice his obedience skills. I love watching him run—beauty in motion. As a trainer I would like to tell people to love their dogs like a member of the family, be consistent, and be the leader of their pack.

M. POKEY P'DOOH
NEW YORK, NEW YORK

P okey, a small white French Poodle presently residing in Manhattan, was walking with his daddy when he slipped his leash. Everyone searched for Pokey. His daddy, Al, went upstairs to get his passport so he could flee the country before Princess, Pokey's mother, found out. The elevator door opened and there was Pokey! He had come up twelve floors alone in the elevator and was waiting for Daddy. Last year, Pokey won the Mayor's Cup for "Smartest Dog" in Manhattan, went to dinner at Le Boeuf, and there was dancing in the street! Everyone loves little Pokey.

MAC
AURORA, COLORADO

"The Mac Attack" weighs about eighty pounds, has a tail like a whip (capable of shattering glass), and is black and white as if he's wearing a tuxedo! His favorite hobbies are long walks and chewing and chewing and chewing. Don't get me wrong, he's not a naughty dog—he just likes to chew! Every bit of his eighty pounds is lovable and makes life more exciting!

McGeorge Bundy Powers
MIDDLEBURY, CONNECTICUT

McGeorge was born in late September of 1982. Since the day of his birth, he has given our family immeasurable pleasure. He seemed to know that he belonged with us from the very start of his life. He has a wonderful smile and greets everyone with it. The only time he looks unhappy is when he sees our luggage being packed. We call it his "suitcase face." He refuses to acknowledge us until we are safely home from our travels. We are always as elated to see him as he is to see us. We love this wonderful dog.

MCNABB'S NOBLE CHAN
OBLONG, ILLINOIS

Chan is a seventy-four-pound cinnamon Chow, born November 12, 1982. He is extremely friendly and loves anyone who will feed him cookies. He generally lies around the house, but in the summer he likes to lie under a large walnut tree and watch the grass grow. His favorite food is chicken, but he won't turn other goodies down. He likes to go for a ride in the car once in a while. His favorite TV show is *Empty Nest.*

MEDDLESOME MATTIE REICHERT
FRANKLIN, INDIANA

Meddle loves to eat. Her favorite food is Munchkins from Dunkin' Donuts. A Dobie Shepherd, shiny black with brown socks and a white neck, she is great at digging and once excavated a part of the garage. She got her name because she is always into something. She likes snowballs, Dairy Queen, and going to the drive-thru window to pay the electric bill because they give bones to dogs in the car. Meddle was my Mother's Day present ten years ago, when she was only five weeks old. Oh yes, she loves balls that make a whoosh sound when you bite them.

MANDY HABERCHAK
PITTSBURGH, PENNSYLVANIA

Mandy, who was born in August 1992, is a black-and-white miniature Toy Poodle. Grandma describes her as a "lovable holy terror." Constantly on the go, she chews up anything she can find, digs up the flower beds, pulls vegetables off the plants, and eats the bread crumbs put out for the birds. Mandy enjoys her naps on top of the pet rabbit's cage and insists on stealing the rabbit's blanket.

MARGEAUX FRANCESCA CUMMINGS
LAS VEGAS, NEVADA

Margo is a beautiful and happy two-year-old fawn-and-white English Bulldog. She is devoted to her master, and her favorite activities include playing with her bulldog friend, Adam, and chewing her bones. She also gets great joy out of chewing on her master's shoes as she and her master walk through the house. Margo likes to sleep late, but immediately upon waking she goes outside and barks to let the whole world know she's up and it's time for another fun day!

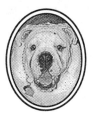

MARTY SKAFI
HOUSTON, TEXAS

Marty is a nine-pound, black-and-tan male Miniature Pinscher. He became part of our family in August 1983. At first he was content to let our female Miniature Pinscher do all the guard work. Then one day, while walking in the park, a man came running toward us and Marty almost ate him alive. Since then he patrols the yard and house, stopping by long enough for a hug and a kiss, then back to work. He has been a great "mother" to our various litters; he answers puppy cries and checks to see all is okay.

MAX-A-MILLION CHESAPEAKE KELIHER
DALLAS, TEXAS

Max arrived, wearing a bow, for Christmas 1991. He quickly began to retrieve everything in sight, including a pair of wire-rim eyeglasses that he brought downstairs, wagging his tail excitedly. The glasses survived, and Max moved into a house with a big yard to run around in. Max went to obedience school, where he was the funniest if not the most trained pupil. He now spends his days swimming, supervising the yardman and housekeepers, chasing tennis balls, announcing visitors, keeping the foot of the bed warm during winter nights, and bringing joy, love, and happiness to his family.

MAX PHILLIPS
NEW YORK, NEW YORK

Max is a small black dog who lives at South Street Seaport on a schooner. He thinks all dogs live on boats. He spends his days keeping watch over historic ships, chasing sea gulls, or lounging around on deck. Even though he was the runt of a litter of mutts, little Julia thought Max was perfect. The summer Max sailed to Nova Scotia, he saw his first whale. He was confused about whether to bark or hide. Though most at home on his sea legs, Max leaps four feet into the air at the mere mention of the word "park."

MAX TEVINGTON
JACKSONVILLE, FLORIDA

I adopted Max, a black-and-tan German Shepherd, from a German animal shelter (Tier Heim) two years ago. He is a retired East German Border dog who worked at the Berlin Wall for eight years. He has been on Channel 4 in Jacksonville for the anniversary of the Berlin Wall coming down. Max likes to chase frisbees and go for walks. His favorite food is canned salmon. When he hears thunder, he tries to build a nest in my closet with pantyhose I keep in a basket. Max likes sailing and air conditioning, and never experienced fleas until he moved to Florida one year ago.

MAXINE CYMRU AM BETH
MIDWAY CITY, CALIFORNIA

Maxine is a three-and-a-half-year-old brindle Welsh Cardigan Corgi. She is a serious worrier as she guards the world. She quickly earned the nickname "Stuffy" as she fussily mothers her family. She loves to be petted and will slide her nose under your hand; then, with a flip, she'll toss your hand so it lands on her head and you may proceed with the petting. She sleeps lovingly on a pillow at the head of the bed so she can rest a paw on each of the persons she owns as she guards us through each night.

MAXWELL SHORT
NASHVILLE, TENNESSEE

Max is a large, beautiful, clumsy Samoyed puppy who delights in the most simple pleasures of life. Leaves, butterflies, and water sprinklers fascinate him. He sleeps on his back near the front door so he can be the first to greet any arrivals. Max has rather unusual dietary habits. He has consumed eyeglasses, pantyhose, socks, parts of a teddy bear, a beanbag lap desk, and an entire box of checks. Max smiles constantly, loves to cuddle, and is a continual source of amusement to the people he owns.

MERENE'S ISLE OF CAPRI (CAPRI MEITZLER)
ALLENTOWN, PENNSYLVANIA

Capri is a five-year-old white Miniature Poodle. Her grandmother was in the movie *She Devil*. Capri loves to play ball by herself for hours at a time. She hides the ball, then finds it. She pushes it down the cellar steps and brings it up again. Outside she pushes it through the nylon of the lounge chair, retrieves it, and repeats her actions. Finally I take it away so she can rest. She is a fun-loving dog and likes everybody.

MICKEY HEINLEN-GLAVIANO
LAS VEGAS, NEVADA

Mickey is a fifteen-year-old longhaired Dachshund and Chihuahua with a black body and white face, and tan and white legs. Jr. and Opal got him when he was a puppy and took him to Zapata, Texas, from Colorado when they retired. He sits up, shakes a paw, and sings. He once rescued a starving black kitten. Jr. brought him to us from Denver on an airplane. When you tell Mickey that Jr.'s coming back, he goes outside and watches the airplanes as they land at the airport. If you step close to him, he barks to let you know he's there.

Miles Fett
ROCHESTER HILLS, MICHIGAN

Our Border Collie, Miles, has a strange obsession with tearing up cardboard boxes. He literally attacks boxes! Miles can turn a three-foot-square box into a pile of bite-size cardboard pieces in three or four minutes. He likes to have a box every day, so we've become great box hunters. We watch for new neighbors moving in, because soon after they arrive, boxes get tossed out for the garbage truck. The stock people in stores love us because we regularly clear the shelves of empty boxes. You'd think we've been given a piece of gold when our friends give us boxes they've saved for Miles.

MINKA PRATT ELLIOTT
NOBLEBORO, MAINE

Minka is probably the naughtiest dog alive. Being part Basenji, she doesn't bark. She screeches! She jumps straight up in the air—a trick that gets her on the counter to eat the cat food. Chewing is her favorite pastime. She has chewed holes in quilts, couches, pillowcases, and eyeglasses. Minka bears *no* shame when caught in the act. Even so, I love her very much. She has character, integrity, and guts. When I think of Minka, I am reminded of a candle. She brightens my life and brings warmth to my heart.

MISCHIEF (TROUBLE) VERSECKES
PASCAGOULA, MISSISSIPPI

Found on a busy street, then sent to a shelter, she was saved the day before death. This white Maltese is a bouncing, happy, "can get in trouble at the blink of an eye" little girl. She'll jump up, grab the hem of your shorts, and, if they're loose, yank them down to your knees. With her little paws she will give you a good back scratch and while she's at it comb your hair with her teeth. In the one and a half years we've had her, we've become attached and have come to love this bundle of energy.

MISCHKA WALKER
HIGH POINT, NORTH CAROLINA

Mischka (AKC No. NT564804) is a full-blooded red Chow Chow with a heart of gold. While most people shy away from this breed, we have never regretted our choice. But don't ever try to put socks on when Mischka is around! Just as you get ready to stick your foot in, he snatches the sock and defies you to try to get it back. We still love him—even if it means wet socks with lots of holes in them. Our house would not be a home if we didn't have him to share it with us. Thank you, Mischka!

MISS AUGIE CRUSAN
SURREY, ENGLAND

Miss Augie was born in a small town in Somerset, New Jersey. She later moved to Long Island, where she was quite happy until . . . *"the move"!* (That is how she terms it.) She was forced to endure six months of quarantine in England. Freedom finally came, and now she lives in a quiet English home in Surrey, England. She plans to retire to Orlando, Florida. In the meantime she spends her time learning how to bark with a proper British accent. Miss Augie lists her birthdate as August 1, 1979. (Sadly, Miss Augie died two days before her return to Florida, June 1992. She is greatly missed.)

MISS JANE MARPLE CARLSON-RASIE
INDIAN NECK, CONNECTICUT

Brilliant, effervescent, creative, and eccentric best describe Miss Jane Marple, our housemate of thirteen years. A rock collector of indiscriminate taste, she was the inventor of Hoop Tug of War and in her younger years a gymnast who could do a somersault in the air while simultaneously catching a frisbee (photo-documented). One neighbor describes Miss Jane Marple as the wonder dog with many Pet-degrees. She is loved by eccentric *Homo sapiens* who allow Marple to select her own Christmas gifts and profess she speaks English with all the proper inflections.

MISS KIWI WARD
CLEAR LAKE, MINNESOTA

K iwi is a Miniature Schnauzer of a solid silver color. She is a ferocious watchdog. Any creature that dares to venture into her yard is in grave danger. She does some of her guarding from atop her owner's house via trees, ladders, or anything available to climb on. Her most favorite thing is to go fishing in the boat and diligently watch the bobbers to let you know when you have a fish. Then she'll hang over the side, pull the fish into the boat, and hold it in her mouth until the hook is removed.

MISS T WU
HUNTSVILLE, ALABAMA

Miss T is a seven-year-old Shih Tzu, silver and white, extremely friendly and gentle. She stands up on her back feet and nods "yes" when you ask if she wants bologna. (She will only eat Oscar Mayer brand.) When she is ready to get out of the swimming pool, she swims over to the ladder and climbs out. She likes to have a bath and holds her head so soap doesn't get in her eyes. She wears Passion perfume with her hair on top of her head in two ponytails with bright bows. Miss T's masters are Sue and Bob Lipscomb and daughter Christina Briseno.

MISSY "MISS MUPPHET"
RANCHO CUCAMONGA, CALIFORNIA

Missy is a black Cocker. She loves to play with her toys, and most of all she loves to eat. She once saved her little friend, Scruffy, from drowning in the family pool. He was a blind Cock-A-Poo and very old. He accidentally fell in, and Missy ran in the house and barked until her owner came to see the other dog in the pool. Her owners feel she is a real heroine. She saved his life. Missy is a very special dog.

MISSY ST. CLAIR
PRINCETON, WEST VIRGINIA

Missy is an adorable and intelligent Yorkshire Terrier born July 16, 1986, and owned by Dr. Thomas and Denise St. Clair. Missy has an extensive vocabulary. Her favorite words are "go bye-bye" and "bicycle." She loves to ride in her special carrier with her dad. Missy is always a source of joy and entertainment. Once when we were traveling in the car, we passed through an area that had a strong skunk odor. Missy was lying in her dad's lap. She raised her head and sniffed, looked at her dad with pure disgust written on her face, and promptly got up and moved.

MISTER BAXTER PRAVDA
CORAL SPRINGS, FLORIDA

Mister Baxter is a brown-and-white Boxer who enjoys life in sunny Florida. He's partial to drive-in movies, chewing on a plant named Norman, and playing with a squeaky toy named Hedgehog. He's a playful pup who loves attention, but when he's sleepy there's no waking him up and getting him off the couch. Mister Baxter has floppy ears, pink toes, and a tongue that loves to kiss. He is referred to as simply "the boy" by his human parents, Jodi and Scott. The boy hopes to travel north to meet his cousins Humphrey and Uncle Bo.

MITZI JANE WILLIAMS
RENO, NEVADA

Mitzi Jane is a six-year-old, twelve-pound Miniature Pinscher. She is exceptionally intelligent and doesn't sleep much during the day because she's afraid she may miss something. Her T-shirt has HERE COMES TROUBLE on it, which is most appropriate. When the telephone rings, she barks and runs to it. She also barks to alert me to an uneven load in the washing machine—she learned to help me on her own initiative through acute observation. Mitzi is lovable yet a good watchdog. She may be obnoxiously active on occasion, but what a wonderful companion!

MITZI MITZELFELT
INDIANAPOLIS, INDIANA

Mitzi is a purebred Cocker Spaniel who was born on February 17, 1991. She is blonde with beautiful white markings on her paws, head and neck area and weighs in at 28 pounds. Extremely intelligent, friendly and very faithful to her owner, Mitzi's favorite snacks are pizza and ice cream. She loves to play catch, take walks, go for car rides and especially visit her "Grandparents" Nancy and John. Everyone that meets Mitzi wants to take her home.

M'LADY-BONNIE OF INWOOD
MONTCLAIR, NEW JERSEY

M'Lady-Bonnie of Inwood is a liver-and-white English Springer Spaniel (AKC). She is a youthful, stylish, mannerly, eleven-year-old dame who shared her loving "sporting" life with the late Sir-Skeeter-Clyde of Inwood. She is from a line of "Bench" Champions and whelped eleven puppies her first time. Lady is very social. She likes to take her red leash in her mouth and proudly, with great accomplishment, lead herself home from the park to lounge with birds and squirrels on her home grounds.

MOJAVE BROWN
SOUND BEACH, NEW YORK

Mojave, a tail-whipping, big, friendly yellow Labrador, came to live with my brother's family fourteen years ago. Whenever we phoned back east, we'd spend much of the time talking about his antics. The best stories came around the holidays when he'd wander through the dining area, stealing and eating everyone's napkins. A true water dog, he and a female companion were nearly thrown in jail for taking a dip in a public park lake. Mojave's gone now, but it's easy for me to picture him in dog heaven, lying in the grass, chewing on someone else's napkin.

MOLLIE BEA SCHULZ
ARLINGTON, TEXAS

Mollie is a ten-year-old, solid-black Cocker who takes her guard duty very seriously. The only problem with that is that she guards empty sacks. I think this has something to do with her weight problem. To put it mildly, she is as broad as she is long. She knows that food comes in sacks; therefore, if there is a sack within a twenty-mile radius, she'll guard it from her three sisters for fear she won't get her fair share of the food.

MOLLY BICKLEY
LEAWOOD, KANSAS

Molly, a four-year-old West Highland Terrier, is best described as a lovable, short white bundle with a sweet disposition. Molly enjoys meeting everyone, and her favorite trick is "high five." She takes her job of squirrel patrol very seriously and will camp noiselessly under a tree for hours while protecting her master's home from the dreaded beasts. Molly is an avid mountain hiker and is the social "Westie-Woman" of her neighborhood. She delights everyone who meets her.

MOLLY FULTON
CHICAGO, ILLINOIS

Molly is a white Lhasa Apso owned by Barbara Fulton and Paul Rossberger. A Chicago native, she enjoys her walks through Lincoln Park as well as socializing with her many neighborhood friends. Molly recently broke her leg during an ill-fated rabbit chase while visiting in the suburbs. Her dad now affectionately refers to her as "The Bionic Dog" because of all the elaborate surgery she has endured. It is feared that she is planning a revenge scheme against the rabbit à la *Fatal Attraction*. Usually a very sweet dog, she has never met a person or a scrap of food that she doesn't like.

MOLLY LOUISE LARABEE
NACOGDOCHES, TEXAS

Molly is a 107-pound Golden Retreiver/ Black Lab. Since she would rather be petted than eat, we attribute her weight to her big heart. She loves people, chasing jets and thunder across the sky, and cold water. At ten, she still has puppy ways, delivering odd things to our door: a pillow left on a tractor seat, a six-pack of beer, a sack of rocks, whatever attracts her in the midnight hour. She is true and loyal and always makes me smile, even when I have to scold her.

MOLLY ORR
ARLINGTON, TEXAS

Molly Orr, a Sheltie, resides with Pat and David in Arlington, Texas. Every morning at six, she enthusiastically pulls the covers off David, then coerces him into taking her for a car ride around the neighborhood. She accomplishes this by laying her head across his chest and staring at him until he capitulates. Molly loves to watch sports on the big-screen TV, sing, perform tricks (she says *mama* clearly), "help" David unpack after trips, and listen intently to conversations, extracting and responding to familiar words. Occasionally she answers the phone by removing the receiver when it rings.

CH. MONAMI ARTEMIS— ("SPIFFY")
ALAMEDA, CALIFORNIA

There are few things I enjoy more than simply being with my Spiffy. It's so easy to make her happy; when she's happy, she is absolutely *thrilled.* I make sure we have at least one adventure every day—some adventures are bigger than others! Spiffy is very aware of my presence—or absence. She is always "there for me." A glamour girl, Spiffy is a typical Belgian Tervuren. She has a true working Belgian temperament: attentive and observant, somewhat independent but responsible. A trusting and trustworthy friend, Spiffy *knows* she's special.

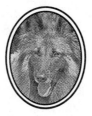

Montego Bay Sudden Splash
RYE BROOK, NEW YORK

Monty was a Yorkshire Terrier, the sweetest four and a half pounds, with a doll face. People thought she was a stuffed toy when I carried her tucked under my arm, then she would move or blink an eye and they would remark, "Oh, it's real!" She got her name because when I went to pick her up at a dog show, it had rained heavily that day and the tent had pockets of water. Someone pushed up the side and I got drenched, head to toe, with rainwater.

MOOSE COULEHAN
EL PASO, TEXAS

Moose, a 170-pound St. Bernard, loved peanut butter but hated snow despite her Alpine background. She surveyed the world happily from her favorite perch atop her owner's roof, which she reached by lumbering up the back outside stairs—except in snowstorms. Alarmed pedestrians, motorists, and even a police officer rang the doorbell to warn: "There's a *big* dog on your roof." Cancer toppled the brown-and-white pet from her lofty post at the age of six. Because of her size, she was ungainly, but a devoted, happy dog—until the snow started.

MORGAN ALONSO
LOS ANGELES, CALIFORNIA

Morgan is a survivor of the '94 California Earthquake. Alone and trembling, he was adopted by Vivian and is working on his abandonment issues. Morgan is very affectionate. He will be two in November, which makes him a Sagittarius, a sign associated with free spirit. Morgan proved this one night by working till 3 A.M. in his newly fenced yard. He escaped early next morning and wants to know if Clint Eastwood is interested in filming his story. A sympathetic confidant, his reply to the most shocking of crises is to flip over so you can scratch his belly.

MORGAN MUNDANE PALMER
PEWAUKEE, WISCONSIN

Morgan is a beautiful twelve-year-old Airedale with the energy of a puppy when he's not sleeping. He is very friendly even when little children try to ride him. Morgan does have days of not feeling so well, like when he ate a rug and it started to expand in his stomach. Luckily Mom is always there for him. Other exciting times consist of trying to eat my cat, dressing in a bow tie and coordinating sweater for our wedding albums and Christmas, and eating cheese. His favorite days are Christmas and birthdays because he loves to open presents.

MORTON R. NUGENT
JAMISON, PENNSYLVANIA

Mort the Sport is a mix between a New-foundland and Labrador, roughly eight years old and very agile. Mort keeps a slim figure, weighing in at 130 pounds. He's very distinguished-looking with his gray hair and deep black coat. Mort is very protective, not nice to strangers, but he sings to friends. Whenever there is a large gathering, Mort takes pride in clearing out a room within seconds. He keeps humans on the run with his aroma therapy. But don't underestimate his charm—he's lived with two female dogs and one female cat.

MOUNTAIN LAUREL'S MACKENZIE
MANCHESTER, CONNECTICUT

MacKenzie was born on February 11, 1992. She is a rare native American purebred Chinook. There are about 300 registrable Chinooks in the world. Her ancestors were originally from New Hampshire and were sled dogs who traveled with Admirals Byrd and Perry. She spends part of her day practicing for obedience and breed training. She has achieved to Novice level for shows. She enjoys classes and does well. MacKenzie and her owners Phil and Laurel Morrissette hope to travel to Rare Breed, Fun Matches and UKC shows in their area. We hope to be good ambassadors for all Chinooks.

MR. DOOLITTLE
SOUTH RIVER, NEW JERSEY

Born on August 17, 1987, Mr. Doolittle is a rambunctious blue and tan Yorkshire Terrier. Doo enjoys taking walks, frolicking in his yard and pool, hiding under the bed and nipping your feet should they get too close, and shopping at the nearby pet store. Mr. Doolittle is a fashionable little fella who's professionally groomed biweekly and enjoys a full wardrobe—everything from shirts to sweaters (knit by Granny) to denim overalls and a surfing outfit. Doo is extremely bright and orderly: he can fetch as well as toss small toys which he stores in his fire hydrant toy box.

MR. PIERRE MACKEEVER
BANNING, CALIFORNIA

MacKeever is a three-year-old male Bichon Frise. His favorite activities are putting on his sun visor and going for a ride in the car, and running through the house playing with his toys. He really loves it when sometimes he gets to eat corn off the cob! He carries his rawhide bone and toy mouse wherever he goes. When you mention the words "comb your hair," he runs and hides. When you sit down to watch TV, he wants to lie beside you and have his chest rubbed. He says he has the best parents in the world!

MUFFY ("BABES") HINCK
ST. CHARLES, ILLINOIS

Muffy is a six-year-old, buff-colored Lhasa Apso. She is the boss of *all* in her house (especially Dad, Roy). Muffy loves to show off how beautiful she is by rolling and kicking her legs in the air and snorting. To stay so beautiful, Muffy needs lots of beauty sleep. Anytime she can find a place to make a "nest" or snuggle up or get under the covers, she sleeps! Muffy is very possessive with her dog treats and "buries" them all over. She even once hid one in her Dad's suitcase that was later discovered while on vacation!

MULLIGAN (COLLINS)
SHERMAN OAKS, CALIFORNIA

Mulligan is our pure breed Golden Retriever from Champion lines with a temperament every dog should have. He is beautiful, regal and loves to swim. Mulligan will swim for hours as long as he is with someone he loves, and that someone has a tennis ball. After a day of swimming, he can be found in his home-made cave (built by Mulligan of course!) in the ivy bushes in the back yard.

MUNCHIE McNULTY-ASHCRAFT
APOLLO BEACH, FLORIDA

Munchie is a Terrier/Sheltie mix who is eight years old. She's red and white, and looks more like a Sheltie than a Terrier. She's the proud mother of three (one who also lives with us). Munchie always wants to be a mother. She has several false pregnancies a year, and during these times she steals our cordless phones and remote controls and tries to nurse them. She also has nursed two almost full-grown male cats. She's the "Queen" of our house. She loves to swim, and we can't keep her out of the pool and spa.

MURPHY BRANTON BLACKBURN
MORRISTOWN, TENNESSEE

Murphy is a creme-dilute Shar Pei girl pup. Her given name is "Raisin Creme Sha-Googie Bop," which describes her personality to a tee. Murphy is a compact circus act: a high-wire, double-somersaulting, ever-smiling dog. She finds humor in everything: dancing to the veterinarian's office and laughing during bathtime. Her favorite game is Stair Queen. At the top of the stairs, in a crouched position, she waits for her four fellow Shar Pei pals to climb up. If they make it to the top, she lunges at them, forcing a thunderous avalanche of downward bouncing wrinkles.

MY ICON C.D., A.D., V.B
FOSTER CITY, CALIFORNIA

A field-bred black Labrador Retriever trained in tracking, obedience, protection and narcotics detection, Icon's a tribute to his breed. He's a model in motivation, perseverance and relentless determination. With that "typical spirit and zest for living," he's a survivor of endless medical problems. A monument to the term long-suffering and "just a great lab" . . . he's never given up. Thanks for all that you've taught me and for all the doors you've opened for us.— My undying devotion, as a Mom and a pal. Owner/Trainer, Peggy Amerman Blake.

NEWMAN TCHAIKOVSKI
BEREA, OHIO

He's called Newman because his blue eyes are just like Paul's. He is an eighty-five-pound Alaskan Husky, black and white with Husky markings and Collie size and body. He follows me like a shadow. Newman is a born leader, very passive, loves people to a fault, and can walk away from a doggy argument unless pushed too far—then he knows how to use his muscle. His companion, Wolf, and he are like Siamese twins, inseparable. Newman's summer activity is finding shade or waiting for the air conditioning to come on. In the winter, he is a reliable lead dog in a two-four dog team.

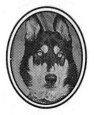

311

NICHOLAS SCOTT
GARLAND, TEXAS

Nicholas, an eight-year-old buff Cocker Spaniel, has become famous to children worldwide who have read his three books, *Too Smart for Trouble, Not Better . . . Not Worse . . . Just Different,* and *Too Cool for Drugs.* He co-authored these with his human, counselor Sharon Scott. His animal friends, dogs Shawn and Mandy and cats Cedric and Katy, give him rave reviews since he mentions them in his books! Nicholas frequently lectures at elementary schools, does volunteer work at nursing homes, and helps at the animal shelter. He is a true example of man's (and animal's!) best friend.

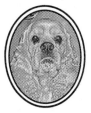

NIFTY ("BUNKIE") BRAUDIS
GREENWICH, CONNECTICUT

Ninety pounds of leaping, tail-wagging energy is surely the best way to describe this warmhearted, six-and-a-half-year-old black Lab. The light of her mom Lee's and late grandma Kay's lives, she has a way of becoming the "lovey" of everyone she meets. Popularly known for her love of ocean swims, bedroom slippers, brush-nabbing, mud baths, and sloppy kisses, Nifty has special eyes for only one person—her mom Lee. Canine speaking, Nifty's best pal is Janey, a mini Lab mix who loves sleepovers and relishes trying to kidnap the limelight. No dog, however, can outshine Nifty.

NIKKI
HONOLULU, HAWAII

Nikki was a German Shepherd who lived in Hawaii with Colonel Hause and his son H.B. Every morning Nikki would go with H.B. to the end of a pier and watch H.B. dive in and swim a great distance to the next pier. Nikki would run along the shoreline and greet H.B. as he climbed out of the water. One day H.B. developed horrible stomach cramps and couldn't continue to swim. Nikki then jumped into the water and located H.B., who was doing the deadman's float. Nikki allowed H.B. to grab on to the nape of his neck and swam him safely to shore. Truly a heroic lifesaver.

NIKKI BRANTON BLACKBURN
MORRISTOWN, TENNESSEE

Anyone interested in having their stamps/envelopes licked for free, please contact Nikki, a black Shar Pei girl. Nikki is a serious licking kind of pup, with hopes of growing up to be a professional postal licker. She licks the floors, the walls, the ceilings. If the wind blows, she licks it. If a cow "moos" in a distant field, she licks the sound. Nikki was once caught licking the top of her own head while balanced on one paw, humming the tune of "I Feel Pretty Licky!" So please, everyone, give Nikki a meaningful purpose—send stamps!

NOAH JOHNSON
THAXTON, VIRGINIA

Noah is a four-year-old black-and-tan German Shepherd cross. A seasoned traveler, Noah was born in Arkansas while his mother, Sterling, was en route to Virginia with her trusted chauffeur and midwife, Phyllis. He is head of security for the farm he and Sterling live on in southwest Virginia. He takes time for his church, especially youth activities, and community affairs, such as pet therapy and fund-raisers for the SPCA. An outstanding athlete, Noah swims, hikes, races with the horses, and catches balls.

NOEL ("WELLY") HANNOLD
LOCKPORT, NEW YORK

Noel is a black Lab and miniature Shepherd mix. Both parents were pedigreed, so I guess in her own way she is, too. She has never thought of herself as a dog, but rather as the ruler of a two-legged household. She gets a supper plate and dessert bowl. Her French fries need ketchup and her chips need dip. Her vocabulary is astounding; she even recognizes some spelled words, much to our frustration! Her favorite things include walking her family, her cow-shaped pillow, taking your seat when you get up, and hogging the bed at night. She's loyal and trustworthy and everyone's friend.

NORWAY MYSTIQUE OF BALI REPKA
COLORADO SPRINGS, COLORADO

Norway, a toy white Poodle, was born October 13, 1992. On December 5, she was adopted by Jane and Ron, who named her after the ship they sailed on during their July 1992 honeymoon. Norway is playful, very loving, and likes to take showers and baths. She prefers to sleep at the foot of her owner's bed. In addition to her puppy food, she especially loves cabbage, lettuce, and fruits. When she hears the deer in the yard, she lowly, but sternly, growls—they could be in her flowers!

ODIN (A.K.A. ODIE, DOG)
B. CORK
ROYAL OAK, MICHIGAN

Odin is a female Lab/Golden Retriever mix. Black in color, she is a gentle, loving dog of fifteen years who loves the woods and chasing the critters, but when in her own backyard protects the squirrels and birds from the neighbor's cats. Her favorite friend is Spook, her black cat playmate in the house. She doesn't mind playing second fiddle to five cats as long as we remember her walks and biscuits. Nowadays she is a little stiffer and doesn't run quite as fast, but she is still queen for a day.

OLLIE LEONARDSSON (A.K.A. ONEE BALONEE PEPPERONI NOSE!)
RINDGE, NEW HAMPSHIRE

Ollie is a three-year-old smooth red mini Dachshund who was born in Nebraska. He was given up by a college student while I was working at an animal hospital. He came with a different name. We let him pick his new name (Ollie) out of a hat with several different names on folded papers. Months later we went to the pet shop where he was purchased to pick up his AKC papers. Chills went up my spine as I looked at the paper and saw that his father's name was also Ollie!

ONI-DON'S BILBO ("PUGGINS")
SAN ANTONIO, TEXAS

P uggins is an AKC-registered Pug who picked me out of a pet store five years ago. He is the picture-perfect Pug, with a short-haired fawn body, a curly-cue tail, and the most expressive black-masked face. Puggins is usually full of cheerful energy, but sometimes he will furrow his brow and show his concern for others in his soulful, dark eyes. He loves long walks, long naps, and sighing at just the right moment. Everyone who knows Puggins loves him!

ONION PELTON
IOWA CITY, IOWA

*C*redentials: B.S. (Busy and Sweet) and official member of the Lucky Dog Fan Club. *Career Objective:* To be a good girl. *Special Characteristics:* Beagle, age nine, soft hair, beautiful ears, dark brown eyes with black eyeliner effect at lid edges. *Holds Expertise in:* Announcing guests; warming chairs and sofas; keeping yard free of rabbits, squirrels, and cats; helping in kitchen and study; sitting and looking on deck and porch. *Personal Data:* Likes to travel, swim, take parents on long walks, take naps, and eat all foods (except Greek olives and onions). Abhors storms and the sight and sound of hot-air balloons.

OREO LIENAU
ALLEN PARK, MICHIGAN

O reo is a five-and-a-half-pound black Poo-dle/"Up North" mix. At age twelve, she stands eleven inches high, including her two-inch ears. In her puppy years, she weighed three-quarters of a pound and resembled the gremlin Gizmo. She loves to play with her pound puppy, golf ball, and rawhide chew, sometimes flinging them around the room when she doesn't get her own way. She will lie in any spot of sun, but prefers her blanket and will cry until it's fluffed to her liking. Since she receives a biscuit every time we leave the house, she usually tries to push us out the door.

ORPHEUM OGILVY
TUCSON, ARIZONA

Orphie was born on Christmas Day, 1986. Of no particular breed, she saved Mary and Dave from eternal loneliness by hopping into Mary's car while crossing a busy street in Phoenix when she was just two months old. Orphie is now their very best friend in the world and brings them great joy. Her brother Pancho loves her, and they run together on the golf course. Orphie is a dear friend to all and has her own brick in front of the theater in Phoenix for which she was named.

OTIS ADDAIR
CALLAHAN, FLORIDA

What a name, Otis! What a dog! He is our first purebred Bullmastiff and our first show dog. Weighing in at 143 pounds, he's a barrel of laughs. Nothing seems to bother him, and nothing gets in his way. He'll just plow right over it and keep going. Full of love and expression, he keeps us smiling even when he's slinging slobber from ceiling to floor.

PALLI CHAPMAN
MADISON, NEW JERSEY

Born in Denver, Palli, a chocolate Labrador, grew up in the Rockies. Named for the popular Pallivencio ski trail, she loves outdoor life. Any water requires a swim, and any trail needs to be explored! When "Mom" Jennifer moved, Palli came east to her "grandparents." Now a true Easterner, she is regal, docile, and has beautiful manners. Palli loves a photo and has a magazine cover to her credit. A good day includes a morning walk with Barney, fetching tennis balls, a head-out-the-window car ride, an egg, and sleeping in her "granddad's" bed.

PANCAKE LUCAS
SEBASTOPOL, CALIFORNIA

Pekingese, Doxie, and Mix, tan, white seat, eleven pounds. Mothering instincts and best licker. Helped save a bummer lamb with her licking. Gently carried an aborted five-inch baby sea lion off rocks. Licked and loved her older counterpart. Courageously chased the pet cockatiel. Worked with developmentally delayed, never sparing of licks, to the giggles and smiles of all. Over the loudspeaker at a golf course: "Would the owner of a brown truck come to the lot, a little tan dog is trying to jump back in!" Now after illness, over fourteen years old, she has slowed.

PANDA BEAR
BLAIRSVILLE, GEORGIA

D aisy's pups were all different—three girls and two boys. We decided to keep the one who planted his feet firmly in the middle of the feeding bowl and out-ate all the others. Since he was black and white and chubby, we called him Panda Bear. We watched the weeks speed by while Panda, gifted with enormous paws and a happy-go-lucky disposition, grew into a beautiful Old English Sheepdog. Born in our bedroom and raised in the kitchen, he is our first "homegrown" dog. An intelligent, loving fellow, he is Daisy's pride and joy.

PANION REED
HIGHLAND, CALIFORNIA

Panion (for Companion) is a city Golden Retriever born in April of 1979. She brings balls and slippers eagerly but doesn't want me to play the organ, pulling down my hands with firm nose taps. Halfway through the obedience school finals, she got her nose stuck in chewing gum and lost all interest in completing commands. However, she scores high with me on companionship! Panion has a twin sister, Porschia, who lives in a more rural area and likes to eat avocados from neighboring groves. Both are good as watchdogs and with children.

PANSY BRECHBILL
CHAMBERSBURG, PENNSYLVANIA

Although Pansy was purebred Australian Shepherd, she never got the hang of herding our cows. One day, our three-year-old daughter walked out our lane toward the road; when we finally found her, Pansy was right in front of her, gently steering her into the field. After that, we didn't much care if she couldn't herd cows. Pansy was a much-loved part of our family for ten years. She supervised the milking in our barn. As she aged, she chased fewer rabbits and stayed in her special porch corner. She is buried in a shady place in our pasture.

330

PANTHER GREEN-LANGFORD
TACOMA, WASHINGTON

P anther is a four-year-old black Lab Retriever. He is spoiled beyond belief by his owners and even by his fellow pet Gabe, the Golden Retriever, who is his father figure and sets up rules that Panther surprisingly obeys. He is busy, likes to explore, and is very alert. Strangers find him intimidating due to his strong bark and his large size. He is really a pushover, loving attention, and becomes jealous if he feels that Gabe is receiving more than his share. Never straying far, Panther will follow you as you go about inside the house or outside. He is very affectionate.

PARRASH MALONEY
CLINTON, INDIANA

P arrash is a seven-year-old white dog with black spots. Half Dalmatian and half Blue Australian Tick, she's very friendly and extremely spoiled. Although she spends a lot of time lounging in front of her fan, she comes alive with frantic tail-wagging when her dad Bob gets her leash out for her evening walk. Parrash is fighting a weight problem but is down from 63 pounds to 51 pounds. Her favorite activities include chasing her ball, playing with her "baby," and begging for diet dog food treats. Bob and Lynette are the proud owners of this beloved pet.

PARTNER STERIN
SAN FRANCISCO, CALIFORNIA

Rescuing him off a freeway at about eight weeks old allowed me to think I had saved his life—but he truly saved mine. Together almost twelve years, I have something to live for, someone I would die for. That nose, those paws, his soft scent in the morning, talking in his sleep, his sense of humor ... He is my love, my life, my "Partner." Not well known to most, he is quite famous among friends and co-workers. I will always be grateful for the privilege of having him as my dog and friend.

PATRICIA ANN CLAMPITT
WOODBINE, IOWA

Eleven-year-old Pat is a black, twenty-pound, "who knows what" mixed breed. She is very loving but also very, very protective. She will give anyone endless amounts of kisses. Her favorite pastime is sleeping, but she also enjoys rides in the car. Pat is a picky eater—the chunks of food she doesn't like, she neatly piles on the carpet next to the food bowl.

PEACHES OLIVER
GLEN EASTON, WEST VIRGINIA

Peaches is a Terry-Poo. She came to us from the county animal shelter. At that time, she was a scroungy but very lively little dog. It did not take her long to win us over. One cute thing she does: when we go somewhere and she has to stay home, she gets a bone and hides it; upon our return, she barks until she shows us where the bone is. She loves to be petted and is a very good watchdog. She goes for a daily walk with her master. We would not trade her for anything.

PeeWee Bonzo Brady
BENNETT, NORTH CAROLINA

P eeWee is a reddish-brown Chihuahua with shoebutton eyes and nose. My husband best describes him as "a bum disguised as a dog, looking for the free ride." In return, he gives us love and entertainment, and makes us aware of when we need an attitude adjustment. PeeWee loves Alpo Liver Bites, and my husband hides them between his toes and makes him go crazy. One time, my husband had a hole in his sock, and Pee Wee thought it was a liver bite and bit the hole. When I call him "Bonzo," he knows it's bedtime.

PEGGY MURPHY
JONQUIERE, QUEBEC, CANADA

Peggy is a six-year-old tan Boxer with a black face mask. She is very good-natured and loves to run in the park when off duty. While on duty she is nursemaid to her eighty-four-year-old mistress, Catherine Murphy. Peggy is very serious about her job. She alerts her mistress when anyone is at the door and when the phone rings. She also does several bedchecks each night and awakens her mistress each morning with a cold nose. Kind and forgiving, she is, however, a formidable guard dog.

PENNY ANTE
CHILLICOTHE, OHIO

Penny Ante is an eight-year-old, black-and-white Cardigan Welsh Corgi. She participated in AKC shows for six years, winning 45 ribbons and Best of Breed in Kentucky. She loved showing and seemed to know when we were going. She always made many friends at shows. Penny is very aggressive and a good watchdog. She will take on any cat or dog, even our Australian Shepherd. She herds everything, from the vacuum cleaner to our racehorses. She is intelligent and responsive to all commands and suggestions. She is named for her father, Jack of Clubs, and mother, Strip Poker.

PENNY NELSON
MERRIMAC, WISCONSIN

Penny, age six, is a darling tan-and-white Toy Fox Terrier. She is very energetic and playful. She surprised her family one day by teaching herself to sit up! She looked so proud as she listened to all the words of praise for her accomplishment. Her ability to strike that pose and remain upright for long periods of time is amazing. Penny isn't happy when I leave for work, but when I return there are plenty of hugs and kisses to make up for the hours spent apart.

PEPPER AND GINGER DONAHOO
SPOKANE, WASHINGTON

Pepper and Ginger are fraternal twin Blue Heeler Sisters, bright, rambunctious examples of nearly perpetual motion, loving and loyal to their master, Don. Their antics provoke endless moments of laughter, agitation, profanity, and affection. Purebred instinct and natural ability lead to hours of herding fun. They will round up horses, children, or farm animals with precision. Seemingly fearful of garden hoses, they kill all they can find. Cookies elicit the best of behavior even when tempers flare, and good marrow bones happify them completely. At home in garden or snowbank, lake or pasture, they're as amusing to themselves as they are to us.

PEPPER ("PEPE LE PEW") KURIAN
POMPANO BEACH, FLORIDA

P epper turned out to be a black-and-white Sheep Tzu. We adopted a Shih Tzu, but then she grew to twenty pounds! Pepe loves to travel, although we must drive to faraway destinations; she is too big to fit under the airline seat, as we had planned. She is full of fun and loves family life, visiting her grandma and grandpa daily. If you don't greet her immediately, she reminds you with something like a yodel: BOW-ROW-ROOOO! Pepe's pet peeve is thunderstorms—she wakes us to bring her into bed and cuddle.

PEPPER RONI ANDREWS
BURBANK, CALIFORNIA

A charcoal gray miniature Poodle, Pepper is described by his mother Max as being "needy." He was adopted on February 5, 1991 from a Poodle rescue shelter. Insecure and anxious at first, Pepper has come a long way thanks to his "analyst" and a loving family. Pepper hates thunderstorms and lightning but loves chasing birds out of the yard, playing with his lamb-wool "babies" and snoozing on the den couch. From the shadows of his dog house, Pepper keeps watch on his home and is the first to announce the arrival of guests.

PETE MUNKERS
CONCORD, CALIFORNIA

Pete is an eight-year-old blue merle Great Dane. At 185 pounds he may be a little overweight, but he loves his dog goodies. He lives with his mother Sara, a harlequin Great Dane, and four cats. He is always considerate of his cats. His days are spent playing with his squeak toys and stuffed animals or sleeping on the couch or our bed. He adores going for walks and riding in the station wagon (because it is air-conditioned). When he has to ride in the van, he controls the speed by hitting the console with his paw if you go over thirty-five miles per hour.

PHILOCTETES COREY
NEW YORK, NEW YORK

Phil was found on a Manhattan street on December 17, 1987. He had almost no hair, was crippled and could barely stand up. He was the skinniest black-and-tan miniature Dachshund I had ever seen. He was scooped up out of the snow and taken to the vet, who said Phil was going to die. That was over five years ago. Phil barks constantly, destroys things (he only has seven teeth, though!), and "goes" in all the wrong places. But he always looks at you with those grateful eyes and spinning tail so you can't help but love him.

PIGDUDE BUTLER
APOLLO, PENNSYLVANIA

Born July 2, 1990, a Cocker Spaniel, longhair Dachshund and Shih Tzu mix, Pigdude stands about fourteen inches tall and weighs approximately thirty-two pounds. He has saddle markings and big, expressive brown eyes. His favorite pastime is eating—spaghetti, salad, and garlic bread being his meal of choice—but essentially anything will do. He will do any one of his numerous tricks to get his favorite dessert, brownies. He customarily loafs around the house until he sees his leash, the car keys, or the family arriving home. He has brought a great deal of laughter and fun into our lives. He is truly man's best friend.

PIPER LORE LEEUWENBURG
OCRACOKE ISLAND, NORTH CAROLINA

Piper Lore Leeuwenburg (a.k.a. "Space Dog") is an eleven-year-old Whippet/Miniature Doberman mix. Despite her age, she maintains her schoolgirl figure by chasing sea gulls on the beach and harassing local felines on Ocracoke Island. As she approaches her golden years, Piper continues to be an inspiration to other dogs, who refer to her as "the Jane Fonda of Canines." Even though she eats red meat in moderation, her favorite food is rare prime rib. She currently is working on a low-impact exercise video for dogs.

PIRATE WHITE
DURHAM, NORTH CAROLINA

P art rogue, part philosopher, Pirate likes to stand very still while waiting for a thought. He's a good-hearted little dog, a Boston Terrier, and likes to visit children in the hospital and eat ice cream from their hands. They like him the best because he licks them in the face and has a black patch of fur around one eye. He makes children laugh, everywhere, even serious little babies like Benjamin.

PISTOL KREKLOW
MILWAUKEE, WISCONSIN

Pistol, a Rhodesian Ridgeback, was stolen from our backyard by a junkman when he was eight weeks old. We knew exactly who had our dog, because he was seen taking him. What ensued was five and a half months of intensive undercover work. Pistol knew he wasn't where he belonged and barked constantly. Thus a nuisance call was placed, and through the City Vector Patrol we were able to retrieve our stolen dog! It was truly a miracle. We now have our beautiful boy back where he belongs. Moral of story: protect your pets and keep them in your sight always!

P.J. LOUTHAN
BATTLE MOUNTAIN, NEVADA

P.J. is a particolor Poodle. She and her family have had a love affair ever since she was three and a half weeks old and curled up in her mistress's hand to sleep. She has her family trained to cater to her every want. She likes being pretty, but hates the process of getting that way.

POOH BEAR ALFARO
STANFORD, NORTH CAROLINA

P ooh Bear is known as the Wonder Dog. You wonder what he'll do next. He "reads" his own book when others are reading; gets Kleenex to wipe his nose; gets his leash when he needs to go out; and "argues" if you tell him to "wait a minute." He's a three-year-old Cocker Spaniel who loves to play football, tug-of-war, and hide-and-seek. For two years he fetched our newspaper every day, but lost that "job" recently when he decided to run down the street to play.

POOKANUBA SHEEP CROUSE
CARY, NORTH CAROLINA

Pooky is our lovable Pomeranian with a full red sable coat, fluffy cream tail, and black coloring around his snout. His round brown eyes can melt your heart as he sits waiting patiently for a biscuit treat. He loves playing with a yellow ping-pong ball, flicking it around the room with his catlike paws. He cocks his head to catch every word spoken. Pooky came to our home in 1988 at the age of eight weeks and has been a most loyal companion—plus lapwarmer, unbiased listener, affectionate consoler, and enthusiastic playmate.

PORSCHE ALPINE PENNY DUNN
AURORA, COLORADO

Porsche is the offspring of three generations of champion Cocker Spaniels, yet when Lonnie and Catherine Dunn went to pick up his royal nibs for the first time, he was gnawing a hubcap and covered from head to stumpy tail with car grease. As he approaches age three, his inquisitiveness has never faltered—nor has his quest for dirt or mud in the yard after he's groomed. Despite his sassy, uncouth ways, he's still our favorite pedigree.

POUKY PIERCE
MT. ULLA, NORTH CAROLINA

Believed by breed authorities to be the oldest Tibetan Spaniel in the United States when she passed away in 1993 at age 23, Pouky Pierce will long be remembered. The little red dog scratched at the door when she wanted out and yipped when she wanted back in. If you didn't open the door right away, her vocal outbursts, loud enough to arouse Tibetan monks if trouble was heading toward the monastery, attracted concerned mothers from miles around. Pouky was actually able to speak. She could say "Daddy" and "Bobby" so clearly that she was once mistaken for a child in a locked car!

PRECIOUS LAVENDER
LUCASVILLE, OHIO

P resh is a St. Bernard mix, weighing about 120 pounds. She loves playing in the creek and running through the hills. Her buddies include: Ian, Jon, and Nathan (our sons); Tango and Rio (our cats). She is the most protective yet kindest animal I have ever seen. Every morning, as he leaves for work, my husband tells Presh, "Keep an eye on things, Big'n." She then sits on the top step as if she's standing guard. Nothing comes near our yard without Presh letting us know. She is one animal everyone just adores. Her name fits her perfectly.

PRINCESS GLAVIANO
LAS VEGAS, NEVADA

Princess is a three-year-old brown dog, a big mixed breed. When she was a puppy, she got Chuckie's wallet, opened it, and took out the paper money. If our two cats are out of the yard, she barks until they come back in; then, when they're back inside, she checks them all over to make sure they're all right. When the pet white mice get out, she shows us where they're hiding. Princess loves popcorn. She'll catch it when you throw it, or she'll roll over so you'll give her some.

PRINCESS HEIDI
BOERNE, TEXAS

H eidi, a white German Shepherd, is the principal protector of Robinstone Tower. As obedient as she is wise, Heidi reigns over many exotic animals. Some of the guests have included black buck antelope, deer, rabbits, geese, turkeys, peacocks, and a variety of other fowl. Although she's very brave, she has been known to seek comfort when the weather turns particularly nasty with thunder and lightning. But, to be fair, she is a warm and loving companion, full of grace and compassion, who always wants to be by her owner's side.

PRINCESSA COULEHAN
LIMA, PERU

Princessa, a brown-and-tan German Shepherd born in South America, made both military and canine history. Six of her pups from two different litters became the first K-9 dogs with the Peruvian army. Princessa was gentle but fiercely protective of her owners' offspring. No one entered the family home before she ran her own security check. She died in 1963 and is still mourned by her owners.

PRISCILLA D'NELL BROWN
NEW BRAUNFELS, TEXAS

Priscilla is affectionately called "Pooh Bear" because when she needs her stylist, Diane Mueller, she looks like a tiny white bear. Being four pounds of Poodle aristocracy, she fearlessly maintains law and order over all raccoons (her nemesis), opossums, armadillos, deer, etc., that pass through. Her diet of white chicken meat, garlic hamburger, beef jerky, and fortune cookies at 3:00 A.M. (with TLC) is the bane of Ken Fischer, DVM. Priscilla firmly believes in *everyone* following her house rules. If you don't, you get the Verna Violet look, a scathing down the nose stare that says: "You have stepped in it now!"

PSYCHO WINTER
SAN BERNARDINO, CALIFORNIA

November 1986–August 1992. Psycho was a beautiful fawn-and-white American Terrier Pit Bull. He weighed in at about 150 pounds. My son and Psycho were very close. They did all things together—eating, sleeping, walking, driving. They loved each other. Picture time found Psycho sitting on the patio waiting to have his spike collar, neck scarf, and sunglasses put on. He will be greatly missed, but always loved. I saw Psycho tell Gene goodbye by putting his leg and paw around Gene's shoulder for one last hug. This is in memory of Psycho for my son, Gene Winter.

P.T. FREDERICKSON
GILBERT, ARIZONA

P.T., nickname for Partner Two, is a four-year-old Queensland Heeler. He is mostly black in color with some mottled gray. His favorite pastimes are catching a frisbee and herding cattle while his owner is roping. P.T. enjoys his snack in the evening, which consists of dog biscuits and some doggy ice cream. He's a good watchdog and very protective of his house and owners. He doesn't like being left home, so he gets to travel a lot. P.T.'s not spoiled—just well-loved and a part of the family.

PUPPER DOG JOACHIM
PLEASANT HILL, CALIFORNIA

When rescued, his age was unknown, so "Puppy? or Dog?" created his name. A Sheltie/Pomeranian mix with a heart of pure gold and the face of an angel, he's filled our lives for over twelve years so far. He talks when ignored and walks on two legs for cheese. Age has widened his sleek little body but left his golden heart and graying little angel face intact. In the window every day when I return from work, on the pillow next to me every night, and a million memories in my heart, a better Best Buddy couldn't possibly be created in any way. I love you Pupper Dog.—Mom.

PUTT PUTT AUGER
CONCORD, NORTH CAROLINA

Born a brown-and-white puppy in the spring of 1977, she filled our lives with excitement, wonderment, and love. In the summer of her life, puppy ways yielded to maturity. She filled our lives with protectiveness, acceptance, and most of all love. Now 17, in the winter of her life, time has stilled her voice and left her fragile. We fill her life with caring, devotion, and most of all love. We cherish our brown-and-white puppy.

PYOTE FENSTERMAKER
CATASAUGUA, PENNSYLVANIA

Pyote is a precious seven-year-old white Samoyed with cream coloring. She loves to play and is especially fond of small children. Pyote is very intelligent and knows many vocabulary words such as: bathroom, bye-bye, night-night, walk, and snack. She is so gentle that she wouldn't even hurt a bug. If she sees an ant or spider crawling on the sidewalk, she paws at it playfully and watches it run. In a nutshell, she is quite amazing. We love her very, very much. We wouldn't trade Pyote for all the money in the world. She is absolutely priceless!

QUEEN ANNE II SCHNELL
NEW YORK, NEW YORK

Born November 19, 1990, Annie is a Teacup Yorkie. She was given to her mother, Jean, as a retirement present by the friends and employees of Goldman Saks. It was love at first sight. Jean spends her days nurturing Annie, her third and youngest child. Annie is more human than animal and is currently learning to talk. She and Jean are inseparable. They eat, sleep, and enjoy activities together. Annie was the best thing that ever happened to Jean. We all love her.

QUINCY LOTT
HOUSTON, TEXAS

Quincy is a six-pound Yorkshire Terrier full of spunk. He likes stalking "wild game" such as squirrels, birds, toads, and kitty-cats in his backyard. He never catches anything, but he enjoys the hunt. He loves checking out his stocking at Christmas, and opening presents is fun—whether they're yours or his. Playing with toys and chasing balloons are two of his favorite pastimes. Favorite meals include breakfast, lunch, dinner, and snacks. Any food good enough for humans is good enough for Quincy. He is a loyal, loving, and wonderful pet. We love you, Quincy!

RAISIN
BUELLTON, CALIFORNIA

Raisin is a pudgy black miniature Dachshund, four years old, with expressive brown eyes. On "chew bone day" she can't enjoy her treat unless she has everyone else's. When we've given our dogs their chew bones, she raises a false alarm, running outside to bark hysterically at some nonexistent image; once all the dogs have joined her, she dashes inside, stacks all the chew bones in front of her, and guards them with vicious growls. The other dogs never catch on. Although she is tiny, she is the bravest of all and even chases horses who have the audacity to enter her private space.

RAJAH COLLINS
SHERMAN OAKS, CALIFORNIA

Rajah is our mystery breed. There have been many speculations as to what he is, but no one is sure. We found Rajah on our front porch. He was hungry and cut on his paw, but with some puppy biscuits and a little peroxide he was here to stay. Rajah has the energy of 1,000 dogs. He loves to talk, gnaw on your knuckles, run around the yard in circles, and climb on your lap without you knowing. Rajah weighs about 40 pounds, but he's mastered the art of displacing his weight so he feels like five pounds on your lap.

RAJAH FENNER
SAN FRANCISCO, CALIFORNIA

A male Shepherd/Husky adopted from the SPCA, Rajah is truly Dad's pal. Though he tolerates the Mrs., his routines are very one-sided. His cocked head and big eyes tell time for dinner and walks: the highlights of his day. During walks, his native temper flares when passing small dogs and his leash is strained. Small dogs are simply not tolerated. Larger dogs receive challenging stares and quiet acknowledgment: a gentlemen's agreement. Besides using his own patio for personal ablutions, he is very well-mannered and behaves like a trained seal.

RALPH MARMADUKE CREAMER
MURFREESBORO, TENNESSEE

R alph was part Chow/Husky/Wolf. He was a caring animal who took good care of our family. Ralph was about thirteen years old when he died in 1993. When it snowed, he liked to lie *under* the snow. He always knew when one of us was ill and would lie down beside us. We loved him—he was faithful and we are lonely for him—does this ever go away? He had a cat friend and she misses him, too. We all were inseparable. We all lived together happily!

RAMBO GOLDSTEIN
PRINCE FREDERICK, MARYLAND

Rambo, a very burly red Akita dog with white feet and a black masked face, has been admired by all since he was a puppy. His presence attracted so much attention that his owner, who was in politics, took him along on her campaign for public office. While Rambo rode in the front seat of the car and shook paws, supporters handed out flyers and dog biscuits! Rambo's pawprint designated the checked ballot box and his owner earned a central committee seat! His cousins in Japan were once hard at work in pairs, hunting bears.

REBEL ("MO") ATCHISON
BIRMINGHAM, ALABAMA

Mc is a very handsome solid-black German Shepherd born on May 28, 1981. He is a wonderful watchdog and very protective of his loved ones. Mo lives in the house as an important member of the family, and spends most of his time with his sister, Tiny (Dixie), and mom, Sandy. His favorite activity is going for rides in his car, the Mo-Mobile. Every year he attends the "Blessing of the Animals" service to celebrate St. Francis of Assisi Day. Mo feels he lives a wonderful life because he knows he is very much loved and appreciated.

RED BARON SCHWENK
HOUSTON, TEXAS

Baron was a large red Doberman Pinscher (106 pounds). He liked lots of attention and wanted to play with whoever came to visit. If we ignored him, he would get upset and chew his blanket. He loved to travel and would lie on the folded-down seat of our four-door pickup, which was *his* seat. He didn't like sharing it, not with things or people, and he would let you know it. He was never mean, and I wonder where the Doberman got a bad reputation—it couldn't have been from anyone who had one!

REED'S JOCKO MACKINSEY-ANGUS
SWARTZ CREEK, MICHIGAN

Jocko is a black Scottish Terrier, born February 18, 1989. He was a retirement gift to his master and they go to breakfast every day together. He has traveled the states with his family and is very well behaved, allowing him to stay in some of the best motels. Jocko loves to be outside for long walks where "Oh, what a cute Scotty Dog" is heard constantly. He looks you directly in the eyes and loves conversation—tries to talk. He exhibits a strong and likable personality. He has his own toy box and loves to play soccer with his basketball.

RESKA PANTALL
ROANOKE, VIRGINIA

R eska is a proudly unregistered Dalmatian born on St. Thomas in the U.S. Virgin Islands. She has just recently relocated back in the United States with her owners and ferret sisters, Tiki and Lucy. Reska spent her first two years in Wet Willy's, her owners' restaurant in the Caribbean and has many charismatic traits and talents. One of her best is sniffing out golf balls on the driving range where she takes her walks. The revenue raised from the hundreds of balls she's found has paid off almost all her expenses!

RILEY BARCLAY
HUNTSVILLE, ALABAMA

This little eight-year-old bundle of fluff (some might call it fat) is part Poodle and part Cairn Terrier. Riley may not be the smartest dog around, but what he lacks in that area he certainly makes up in personality. An obedience school dropout (actually it was suggested that he leave), he loves everyone, especially anyone who will play catch with his rag bone. Riley loves to sleep on top of the air vents, but when anyone enters the kitchen he's right there—just in case something edible should fall to the floor.

RIPLEY VAN WINKLE ("CHOYT") STORINO

WATERTOWN, NEW YORK

Ripley is a tricolor Lhasa Apso born on December 24, 1987. She is well trained and very well behaved. Ripley is a joy to have all year round but especially in winter because she loves romping in the snow, even though she sometimes gets trapped in it when the snowbanks are too high. She loves to get her hair put in a ponytail so she can see; she'll rest her head on your lap until her hair is made beautiful. Ripley is a great dog, and I love her very much.

ROBIN GOOKIN
MIDDLEBURG, VIRGINIA

Robin, a local boy, was born in a barn near Middleburg nearly fourteen years ago. His mother was a Jack Russell Terrier, and although we haven't met his father he must have been a big handsome guy because Robin developed into one of the strongest, best-looking seventy-pound farm dogs around. His favorite activities are being taken for a good run, rubbing in anything foul, and vacationing on Cape Cod. When he can't be with his master and mistress, he goes happily to Fursman's Kennels (the canine Hot Springs), where he is treated like a big shot and has lots of friends.

ROCKY BALBOA SHAMBAUGH
FORT WAYNE, INDIANA

Rocky, age four, is a high-spirited, fun-loving Smooth Fox Terrier. His wavy coat is black and white. Favorite playtime activities include chasing butterflies and sunbeams. In the evening, he bounds around the perimeter of his big fenced yard, pausing briefly to jump straight up in the air and then resuming his run. When it's time to come in, he runs to me with tail wagging and looks at me with beautiful brown eyes that seem to say, "I love you very much, Mom—thanks for loving *me* so much and taking such good care of me!"

Rocky Nelson
MERRIMAC, WISCONSIN

ocky is a four-year-old Kong-size Yorkshire Terrier weighing in at eighteen
pounds. He loves horses, vegetables,
pasta, long walks in the woods, and spending time
with buddies Winston and Duffy. He has received
recognition in the newspaper for his football pre-
dictions and was honored in a celebrity look-alike
contest for resembling Joan Rivers' dog Spike. At
home, he remains constantly vigilant to protect his
family from evil chipmunks. His fondest wish is to
spend five minutes alone with the mailman in a
locked room.

ROCKY WARCHALOWSKI
HACKENSACK, NEW JERSEY

When Adele Warchalowski was about to turn thirteen, her best friend, Jody, asked her what she wanted as a gift. "A puppy!" Adele exclaimed. After weeks of no success, Jody asked God to help her get a puppy for Adele. She prayed hard, and days later a little black puppy came running up to her just as she arrived home from school. After checking the newspaper, animal shelter, and police department, Jody's mother determined that the puppy had no home. From that day forward, Rocky has had a home in Adele's house and heart. Their love for each other is truly indescribable.

ROLLAND LEXINGTON MONROE SIEGEL
PORT JEFFERSON STATION, NEW YORK

Since puppyhood, he's known his own mind. A true "fur person," Monroe sleeps on his back on our bed, insists on being fed from a fork, and smiles broadly when each family member returns home. His favorite food is bread. He will bark once for a specific treat, twice for another, and reject an incorrect one given to him. At 112 pounds, obedience training was a necessity, but he was almost retained in Puppy Kindergarten. This Labrador's claim to fame is a second-place finish in a man-dog road race—he could have won but had to drag his owner.

ROSEBUD WILSON
FULLERTON, CALIFORNIA

Rosie is our family clown. She is a black-and-white Australian Shepherd mix with expressive "people" eyes. Her disposition is wonderful. Rosie's favorite thing is Christmas. She has her own stocking and starts checking it several weeks before Christmas. (Every few days Santa adds something.) When Christmas day arrives, she gets dressed up in a big bow and waits for Santa. When it's time to open presents, Rosie gets her sock (plus anything else she can get her paws on) and starts opening her presents. Her personality has and will continue to bring us much laughter and fun.

ROSEY
MADISON, NEW JERSEY

A Pomeranian who really looks like an orange cotton ball with four legs that stick out. Rosey was brought to St. Hubert's Giralda Animal Welfare and Education Center, Madison, New Jersey, at age four months. Since then, she has become the shelter's second mascot. Her job responsibilities include daily petting sessions by schoolchildren and nursing-home residents. When not working, Rosey spends her time charming the staff in the education office. She knows how to smile and has taught that tooth-baring grin to the other dogs in the office. Her favorite activity is tossing her rubber bug in the air and then pouncing on it.

ROSIE HARVIT
MIAMI BEACH, FLORIDA

R osie is a six-pound Yorkshire Terrier who is trained in crowd control but primarily serves her human friend as a certified, bonded, and licensed companion animal. Rosie's duties include: announcing the arrival of visitors (by barking her fool head off), keeping track of the time (by scratching her dish thirty minutes before each meal time), helping with housekeeping (by making various contributions to rugs and tile), and guarding our king-size bed (by nipping toes that invade her space at night). Best of all, when she's happy she smiles at her friends.

ROUGH DIAMOND OF SILVERDUST
TRUMANSBURG, NEW YORK

Diamond is a yearling Old English Sheepdog who is definitely a diamond in the rough. Often accused of being the dog from hell, she is full of energy and mischief. Her mom is a dog trainer and makes her spend her evenings training and learning some manners. Diamond, however, spends her nights dreaming up more trouble to get into tomorrow, and then acts on those plans when each and every opportunity presents itself. Their joint goal is to turn her into a wonderful companion who can earn some obedience titles, but, says Diamond, "not real soon!"

RUSTY
CASPER, WYOMING

Rusty belongs to all of us—or rather we all belong to Rusty. She currently resides at the Casper Humane Society, serving as ambassador in greeting visitors, a security blanket for new residents, and chief public-relations contact for our shelter. Rusty is a beautiful Irish Setter. She is very old, cannot hear at all, and has a faltering walk. She loves to wander through the shelter, greeting all animals and people. Now, in her twilight years, we are pleased to make her comfortable and attempt to return the patience, love, and care she no doubt gave unconditionally during her young years. We are glad she found us.

SADIE BELLE MILLEN
NATRONA HEIGHTS, PENNSYLVANIA

Sadie Belle Millen is a beautiful liver-and-white Shih Tzu, a twelve-and-a-half-pound bundle of energy who has enriched our family with much love. Sadie loves playing fetch, going for walks, and having her belly rubbed, but her very favorite pastime is to be with people. She likes nothing more than to bring her friends together, and even has one marriage to her credit! An impressive record for this two-year-old "matchmaker."

SADIE IOWA TOVA-LEAH NHOMI DINA CHANA GEFILTE ROSENBERG
WHITE ROCK, BRITISH COLUMBIA, CANADA

Sadie, a Chinese Pug born two years ago in Clarinda, Iowa, has appeared on television and been featured on the front page of the newspaper (which noted that she "looked smart in her matching cap and scarf ensemble"). From her perch on the sofa, Sadie scans her street looking for mailmen and paperboys. Though far from being a couch potato, she has a fondness for TV, particularly *Cops* or any show featuring dogs (as evidenced by hurling herself at the screen). Bubbling with personality, Sadie loves to eat, sleep, and go walkies. Her only fear is the "D" word—diet. She converted to Judaism in 1990.

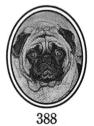

388

SADIE REIMAN
DENVER, COLORADO

Born April 1990, Sadie is a Rhodesian Ridgeback. A well-mannered city dog with an engaging personality, she counts the neighborhood merchants, from dry cleaners to restaurateurs, as friends. Sadie's favorite pastimes include chase and football. A game with myriad variations, chase may consist of running after squirrels or being pursued while carrying a rope that her friends attempt to seize. However, football is her first love. At the scrimmage line Sadie anxiously awaits the quarterback's call of "35-42-hut-hut," whereupon she bounds upfield intent on a quarterback sack. At ninety pounds, she is an effective linebacker.

SAILOR PRIM
MOCKSVILLE, NORTH CAROLINA

Sailor, a two-and-a-half-year-old Cocker Spaniel, is buff-colored with dark freckles across his nose. He is very frisky, chews on your finger like a puppy, and enjoys dry cereal and buttered toast. His favorite time of the day is bedtime. After one last trip outside, usually around 9:00 P.M., he bolts down the hall, leaps on the bed, and situates himself on his daddy's pillow, until he's made to find another spot. He also loves to go for a ride in the car; he sits on the middle armrest, allowing himself a full view of everything.

SALLY
SAN FRANCISCO, CALIFORNIA

S ally is the amazing yellow Labrador Retriever who saved San Francisco. In the middle of the night, gazing through the living room window, she observed vandals dousing a neighbor's parked car with gasoline and setting it on fire. Her fearless, determined barking awakened her owners, who called the fire department just in time to keep the blaze from spreading to a block of row houses. Her heroic deed was written up in the local newspaper.

SAM MOE MARGOLIS
STAMFORD, CONNECTICUT

S am was found wandering the streets of Greenwich. An affectionate white Poodle/ Bichon Frise mix, lean of body and fleet of paw, he flies through Cove Island Park, leaping like a bunny and rousting the squirrels and Canada geese. Initially he would not jump on furniture or beg for food, but he quickly learned the comforts of less restrained breeding. Of the many stuffed animals he inherited, he chose a smaller version of himself, a fluffy pound puppy with black beady eyes named "Son of Sam." He loves to pounce, catch, tug, and chew it. Sam brought me back my smile.

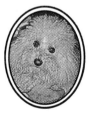

SAMANTHA PORTER FREEMAN
KUTZTOWN, PENNSYLVANIA

Samantha is a five-year-old English Bulldog who used to rule the roost until Spirit (a Bichon Frise) showed up. Samantha loves her, though, and lets her get away with anything. Her personality is the most loving and memorable of any dog you meet. Her favorite things to do are sucking the faces of stuffed animals, sleeping upside down with her tongue out, and chasing corncobs on our walks.

SAMPSON BALLEW GRUMMEL
DURHAM, NORTH CAROLINA

Sam is an eighty-five-pound black Doberman who thinks he is a Teacup Poodle. He is afraid of thunderstorms and brooms. He follows his mom and dad around the house, and does everything his sister does because she got the brains and he got the looks. He sleeps on a water bed and licks us on the face. The Easter Bunny and Santa come to see Sam because he's such a sweet boy. He likes to sing duets with his sister underneath the trees. He is one, and his birthday is October 21.

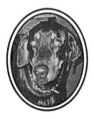

SAMUEL BARTHOLOMEW ROWE
NEW CASTLE, PENNSYLVANIA

I crawled into a pit of mud under a pine tree for Sam'l (*Scott And Mary Lou*), who's half Shepherd, half Wolf. His life began as an adventure when a dairy cow kicked him at fifteen weeks and sent him to a two-day stay at the vet. After he felt he was recovered enough, he sought and avenged his injury on that cow. Sam is very affectionate for his size (130 pounds). He became a very good big brother to his little brother Shadow, a mistreated eleven-month-old pup who learned to trust Sam in every way.

SAMUEL ISAIAH TILLMAN
DURHAM, NORTH CAROLINA

In memory of Samuel Isaiah. Sam was a black Labrador Retriever. He was found in the garbage dump when he was just a puppy. We took him in, and he was the most wonderful companion anyone could ever have. He was so loving and intelligent. He was also quite the hero. Once, Mitzie Gail, Sam's sister, got hit by a car. To protect her from oncoming traffic, he covered her body with his until help came. That's the kind of dog he was. We miss him dearly, but we will never forget him. He will always remain in our hearts.

SARAH SULLIVAN
CHARLOTTE, NORTH CAROLINA

Sarah Sullivan, born in 1990, is a flirtatious West Highland White Terrier. She also answers to Baby, Honey, and Sweetheart. After "spa day," her pristine façade conceals a rambunctious tomboy who prefers squirrel-chasing, garden-digging, and wading in her swimming pool. Her best indoor spot is the lamp table, where she performs serious sentry duty for her street. When bidding for attention, she stares intently into your face and talks. If that fails, she confiscates a bedroom shoe. The end of every day requires a tummy rub. Her VBF (very best friend) is Vivian. Her four-legged buddies are Sassy, Barthley, and Buddy; the two-legged ones are Elizabeth, Will, and Sully.

SARGE
HEMPSTEAD, NEW YORK

A mixed-breed "Shepherd-like" small dog, Sarge was loyal, faithful, and proved himself many times over. One of his most memorable adventures took place when we asked a family member to keep him a few days while a new dog settled in. Sarge started home on his own twenty-plus-mile trek that took him several weeks to complete. He got picked up a few miles from home while checking out the children at an elementary school. We believe he was looking for me.

SASHA ("SASSY") KAMILA COLLETT
ATLANTA, GEORGIA

S assy, a silver-gray Yorkshire Terrier, weighs about ten and a half pounds. A very warm, loving, caring dog, she likes the outdoors and rules the roost. She licks my tears away, gets excited with laughter, and loves to be snuggled under the neck. Sassy is my bird-watcher, house-watcher, and cricket-eater. Her favorite toy is a blue ball that's just about had its day. When she's in her baby mood, she'll gnaw on a baby bottle. She's lowered my blood pressure, cured my moody blues, and given me a new "leash" on life.

SASHA MALIKEI DEPRIEST-CHALMERS
LANSING, MICHIGAN

S asha Malikei DePriest-Chalmers was born September 28, 1990. She has the Beagle body of her mother and the golden brown of her Labrador father with some white thrown in for character. She was the runt of ten, but was the only one brave enough to leave the doghouse to investigate the family who would fall in love with her expressive face and take her home to Lansing. She loves playing tug-of-war, wrestling with her sisters, sitting on the arm of the couch to look outside, and sleeping on her parents regardless of where they are or what they're doing.

SATAN COE
PORTAGEVILLE, NEW YORK

Satan is a black-and-mahogany ten-year-old Rottweiler who thinks he is two. As a younger dog, he hated the water. The only way to get him into the water was to bribe him. Then one day we were floating on the pond on a raft with a rope attached to one side so we could tie it up at shore. Satan decided we had been away from him long enough so he swam out, grabbed the rope, and towed the raft and us into shore. This was to become one of his favorite games. Satan is so special, we could write a book about him.

SCHATZI
BIRMINGHAM, ALABAMA

Schatzi is a Miniature Dachshund of the puppy variety. She is black and red with tan highlights around her face. She has a dominant, vocal personality and is fiercely protective of her territory. She enjoys wrestling with her brother, Schmitty, and her favorite toy is always whichever one her brother has at the time. When she's hungry, she makes it known in a language only Mother can understand. Like many little girls, Schatzi likes to play in her mother's purse and is fascinated by makeup, though getting her nails done makes her cry. Her pastimes include chewing plastic, eating dirt, and de-stuffing her stuffed animals.

SCHOTZIE JACOBER
CLEAR LAKE OAKES, CALIFORNIA

B orn February 9, 1984, Schotzie is an adorable white Cock-A-Poo with apricot and black markings. He lives with Leslie and James and one-year-old "Tig Cat," an American tabby Minx with tiger stripe markings. He loves to sit at his command post in Leslie and Jane's motor home. If they don't stop when he needs a break, or wants out to inspect the scenery, he stares at them, unblinking, until they pull over. Schotzie loves Leslie and Jane, his knotted sock, motorcycle riding, Tig Cat, Cousin Jim Jim, going out in the boat, and steak.

SCHROEDER PRENDERGAST
NEW YORK, NEW YORK

Schroeder is now thirteen years old and was adopted by us when he was two. He is a West Highland White Terrier who has an affinity for sailing on his master's schooner. He has exceptional sea legs and has never been seasick. Schroeder has traveled extensively by air back and forth between New York, Palm Beach, and Europe. He is a chocoholic and attacks candies with rare aplomb. He makes himself quite obvious before dinnertime by talking. His favorite activity is asserting his superiority at twelve pounds over all the larger dogs on Fifth Avenue.

SCOOTER "THE DOG" MENDUS
WYANDOTTE, MICHIGAN

Scooter is a handsome dog! He's a caramel colored Pomeranian/Poodle. He's been our protector and best friend for 16 years now but he will live forever in our hearts. He loves cheeseburgers and his blankets almost as much as he loves us. Scooter does lots of "cute dog" routines and has made many friends. He hogs the bed at night and sleeps in his "cave" under the table during the day. We take him with us everywhere we go—he even came to our wedding! He's the Best Little Doggie in the world ever and we love him very much!

SCOTTY EATON MAYNARD
NASHVILLE, TENNESSEE

Scotty, a Lhasa-Poo, thought he was a Chow. Scotty came into my life one snowy Sunday in January 1980. He became a friend and companion whose constant approval and total devotion were always there for me. Scotty loved hamburgers at the drive-thru, chasing sea gulls at the beach, kittens, and me. His most famous talent was driving the car. When my vintage car quit, Scotty would stand with front paws on the steering wheel while I pushed. On occasion, sibling rivalry was raised to new levels in my home. There are pets, companions, protectors, and supporters. Scotty was all of these. He was loved, and he is missed.

SCRUFFY SCHIELD
RENO, NEVADA

Scruffy is our little Senior Citizen Mutt, with six toes on one paw. She came into our lives through a near tragedy. She was found as a puppy, drowning in the Truckee River. How she got there we will never know, but we are grateful to have her in our life. Scruffy has raised three human children and numerous canine children, including her mates Amber and Angus, two Rottweilers. Scruffy has been known to jump off second-story decks as well as out of moving vehicles. (We thought she was a cat that had nine lives!)

SEEKN BRANTON BLACKBURN
MORRISTOWN, TENNESSEE

S eekn is a black Shar Pei mommy. She is the proud mother of twenty-four babies. She takes her mothering seriously, and all her "kids" keep in touch. But Seekn has another job that she feels is just as important. She is the famous "Scout Queen." Her backyard has a splendid view of the field where the notorious Hill Field Ghost lives—an apparition who slithers into a dog's yard and "slimes" the food and water bowls. Seekn is a fearless scout and always on guard against this fiend. She received the Anti Hill Field Ghost Award for 1991 and 1992.

SEMIDAR ("THE CHOSEN") CULLEN
AKRON, OHIO

Semidar is a black-and-white AKC Siberian Husky. She is my "fluff" moody dog! She loves to be brushed and pays a lot of attention to what kind of hair products one uses. She loves to smell people's hair and their perfume! Anything in the backyard is fair game to her—including birds in flight. She loves to play with my two younger dogs—but only when she's in the mood. Otherwise, she likes to lie on my newspapers next to my recliner. She howls to classical music and enlightens my life tenfold. She always helps me to relax after a very frustrating day.

SHABU SUNRISE
LITTLETON, COLORADO

Shabu is a one-year-old white Labrador Retriever who owns Chuck and Sharlene Gillispie. Shabu loves to swim in nearby Chatfield Reservoir and will play in whatever water is available. He is testing for his Junior Hunter status and promises to do his best to develop Chuck into a great hunting companion. Shabu also spends many hours with the Foothills Retriever Club, in deep theoretical discussions concerning the necessary equipment, training, and procedures for humans. At home, Shabu likes to have his family help him in the garden, especially when investigating the local snake family.

SHADOW CARROLL
MESA, ARIZONA

S hadow chose his best friend out of a group of people who had come that day for puppies. He crawled straight toward the man he had chosen. A cute black wolf-hybrid who looked like a bear cub, he enjoyed taking showers, playing tag, and going to the river. You didn't need to bother throwing a ball. He'd just look at you as if to say, "You threw it, you go get it." He was also very protective, and no animal or person was allowed near until we said it was okay. More than a pet, Shadow was a best friend.

SHADOW MCBADDOW ROWE
NEW CASTLE, PENNSYLVANIA

S hadow was dropped off at our home when no one was there. He had puppy worms and was very fearful. We figure he was eleven months old and weighed fifteen pounds. Because of his early mistreatment, Shadow never grew to full size for a Shepherd cross. Stocky like a Bulldog, he's now five years old and weighs about seventy pounds. Shadow loves his dad, Scott, the first person he ever loved. He and his brother, Sam, love to chase kitties, rabbits, and birds; they also enjoy hanging out in the garage when their dad is working on vehicles.

SHAGS SORRENTI
LAUDERHILL, FLORIDA

Little Shags wandered into our lives in 1983. She simply walked up to me in a parking lot and gave me her paw. I held it and fell in love. Abandoned, sick, and starving, she came home with us and we helped her get well. As our reward, she gave us unconditional devotion that would last all her short life. Of undefined breeding, with large, soulful brown eyes and a perpetually wagging tail, she was God's most gentle creature. She loved games of hide-and-seek, being petted, and being told "All is forgiven" after some misdeed. Shags passed away January 10, 1991. We love and miss her.

SHANNON MAGIERA
FAIRPORT, NEW YORK

Shannon is my Golden Retriever. She's almost thirteen years old, and we got her from Lollypop Farm, the local Humane Society. As a typical Golden, she allows young kids to poke her eyes and pull her tail, all without a word. Her playmate, Thumper, will get on her nerves, but she wouldn't hurt him—just a bark to remind him she's bigger.

SHASTA COLLETTE
REDMOND, WASHINGTON

On March 22, 1982, a purebred Shetland Sheepdog was born. Just three days later, on March 25, a ten-year-old girl received a book about Shelties for her birthday . . . to prepare her for her new puppy! A shy female puppy was chosen by the girl and given the name Shasta. Since that day, Shasta has given much joy to her family. She's loyal, loving, and definitely unique. While most Shelties' ears flop over, Shasta's stick straight up. She spins in circles when hungry, burps, and even knows how to give "real" hugs.

SHAWNCEY MAX OF EARL
NEW KENSINGTON, PENNSYLVANIA

S hawncey Max of Earl drew national attention to himself the windy, bitter-cold night of January 26, 1988. Our ninety-two-year-old neighbor had fallen outside in the snow at 2:30 A.M. and broken his ankle. Shawncey heard his cries for help and woke us up, enabling us to call the police and paramedics and get the man to the hospital. Our newspaper and two television stations carried the story, and Shawncey was eventually presented with the distinguished William O. Stillman award, given to animals or people who perform heroic deeds. Though only nine pounds, Shawncey proved that true heroes can come in any size.

Shayley Renea Ray
MARTINS FERRY, OHIO

Our dog Shay has to be one of the most intelligent dogs on this planet! She's a five-and-a-half-year-old Terrier/Schnauzer who knows over 100 English language words and at least a dozen tricks, including crawling. She can very gracefully walk on her two hind legs across any room, any length! It's a wonder she doesn't drive, considering she goes *everywhere* with us. Shay loves to wear barettes in her hair and get her toenails painted, too. She'll herd any animal that comes her way. She's also a good protector. Shay's the best dog in the whole world!

SHEP KROHN
ATLANTIC, IOWA

Shep was a large Shepherd mix dog who was my constant companion as I grew up on a farm in Iowa. When we played tug-of-war with a rope, he was an easy winner. One January, Shep followed behind the tractor as Dad drove it to town for repair. Along the route, Shep disappeared. The only gift I wanted for my thirteenth birthday was Shep's return. I had not eaten or slept well since he was lost. In early April, a neighbor three miles away phoned to ask if we had lost a large brownish dog. It was Shep! He was the best birthday present I ever received!

SHIRONA HORST
THORNTON, COLORADO

Shirona is a misunderstood Doberman—beautiful in appearance, commanding in presence, and clumsy in nature. From the time she was a pup until she turned seven months, she was selfishly tossed from home to home, each home trying to make her something she wasn't. Although her past presented many annoying problems, all she ever really needed was love and a chance. While she still has a habit of stepping on you, or knocking things over in her path, she does try. But most important, I think she finally knows where home is.

SIMMORE'S GOLDEN SUN "JEANNIE"
DALLAS, TEXAS

Jeannie, a Sheltie, and her owner volunteer at the Baylor Institute for Rehabilitation in Dallas as part of the Pet Assisted Therapy program. She works with patients suffering from strokes, traumatic brain injury, and other neurologic and orthopedic conditions. The patients truly love her wonderful disposition and many "talents." She retrieves and performs various tricks on command. Jeannie's patience and unselfish demeanor also makes for a best friend and companion at home.

420

SIMON BOLIVAR ZACKS
SURREY, BRITISH COLUMBIA, CANADA

Since his birth eight years ago in Hastings, Nebraska, Yorkshire Terrier Simon has dedicated himself to the procreation of the canine species. Truly a profile in courage, Simon is undaunted by the physical size or the unwillingness of the object of his affections. When not charming the ladies, Simon can be found stretched out on "his" hope chest in the sun or "going walkies." Eschewing the effeminate, Simon boldly rejects all attempts to place a bow in his hair, preferring manly sports such as biting mail as it comes through the slot. Hating baths, Simon will, however, lie prone under the hair dryer for hours.

SIR CECIL RHODES DIFRANCESCO
MOORPARK, CALIFORNIA

ecil was born June 26, 1989. He is an eighty-five-pound Rhodesian Ridgeback who shares his home with a twelve-pound gray tabby named Malibu. Cecil and Malibu disagree often, with Malibu beating a rhythm on Cecil's nose with his declawed little paws. When the argument is over, they cuddle together on the sofa, Cecil stretched the length of the sofa with Malibu purring beside him. Cecil is about as lazy as they come, unless you whisper "walk" or his favorite: "Taco Bell." Cecil was awarded his Good Citizenship Certificate on May 17, 1993. He is adored and loved and spoiled by all who know him.

SIR OTIS OF BURKE CAIRNS
BURKE, VIRGINIA

O tis is a registered Cairn Terrier though you would never guess it as he is a down-to-earth guy. His responsibilities include property security—a position he takes very seriously, making a trip around the yard at least twice a day. He is totally aware of the comings and goings of all the creatures in the neighborhood. As a result, they are all respectful of the premises. He has a sack full of tricks and is happy as long as he is with his family. He is the third son, after Scott and Trey, of Susan and Bill Driggers.

SIR PATRICK OF BANBURY
CENTER POINT, TEXAS

Paddy is a beautiful Blenheim Cavalier King Charles Spaniel, eighteen months old, who came to bless the Danton home at the age of nine weeks. He is developing into a most loving and affectionate baby who wants to spend lots of time in his mum's lap being petted. He makes friends with everyone, including the deer, cats, birds, butterflies, and other animals who also live on his ranch. He is learning several tricks, among them how to wipe his feet upon entering the house. He has his own special bed but prefers to sleep under his mum's.

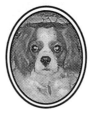

424

SIR RANDI RUFUS
TAMPA, FLORIDA

Randi was our first male Basset Hound, and because of him we will never be without one. He was always full of vim and vigor, and had a deep, beautiful bay. Randi loved to run in our fenced backyard. He didn't even get upset when a mockingbird flew out of a tree and pecked him on his back! Randi was a show dog, but he was just as happy standing outside the ring watching his son, Elmer, take the honors. Randi passed away in November 1986 at ten and a half years of age. We'll always miss him.

SIR ROYAL HUMPHREY HUDSON
WARWICK, RHODE ISLAND

A versatile liver-and-white Springer Spaniel, Humphrey responds equally well to English and Italian commands and has appeared in various fashion magazines. Humphrey is a frequent flyer between Rhode Island, where he enjoys retrieving sticks thrown into Narragansett Bay, and the Italian Piedmont region, where he retrieves Alpine snowballs. He is the self-appointed protector of Tyler, the newest member of the family. We are all reminded that Humphrey is really a dog when he's taunted by Putnam and Dickens, a couple of smart neighborhood cats strutting out of harm's way on the other side of a picket fence.

SIR WINSTON REGINALD DUPREE
BURBANK, CALIFORNIA

Winston was born on July 5, 1985 in Benton, Arkansas (just up the road a piece from the birthplace of President Bill Clinton). After being expelled from obedience school, he began a career in show business by appearing on television as "Winston the Weather Dog." Soon Hollywood called and Winston was lured by the fame and fortune of Tinseltown. He quickly developed a reputation for being "difficult" to work with and his TV career plummeted. A feisty Yorkshire Terrier (or Yorkshire "Terrorist" as his parents David and Max call him), Winston has mellowed and adapted well into a casual retirement.

S.J. MINO KANNER
EAST MEADOW, NEW YORK

S.J. Mino, who departed this earth in December of 1967, was a sable Collie. The family picked her out as a puppy (she was the runt of the litter) because she had to climb over all the other puppies in the litter to nurse. Who could forget this wonderful dog who, as a tiny puppy, got her head stuck between the slats in our picket fence? She was a kind, affectionate, and loyal pet.

SKANSEN'S BLACK MARAUDER ("KAI") TT-84-GSC NITSCHKE
PORTLAND, OREGON

K ai, a six-year-old Giant Schnauzer, is a certified service dog and my co-therapist. He also serves as a trainer for folks evaluating their potential for utilizing a service dog of their own. His trained repertoire includes the full range of canine behavior displays, so he can train or desensitize other dogs (or cats or birds) to a dog under complete control. His other functions include providing "fuzz therapy" to dog-deprived staff at Animal School, Inc., and students at Linfield College. When he is off public duty, he stays at home holding down the couch, watching over his cats, or counting his tennis balls.

SKEEZER MAXX FARRINGTON
NEW PROVIDENCE, NEW JERSEY

Born July 4, 1984, Skeezer Maxx Farrington has a firecracker personality that underscores her tenacious Terrier genes. Her father was a Cairn Terrier, and her mother ... well, was available. Her favorite pastime is playing with one of her vast collection of tennis balls. When her humans started a data services company, Skeezer was appointed Director of Security, responsible for frisking all visitors to check for contraband tennis balls. In recognition of her important contributions, her fellow employees voted to adopt her middle name, Maxx, as the name of a software product and used her likeness as the logo.

SLICK BODINE BRAKEFIELD
COWDEN, ILLINOIS

Slick is an All-American dog, Chihuahua and Dachshund. He's a trucker dog of fourteen years, with a million miles under his collar. His brown hair has turned to white, he has no teeth, and his hearing has faded, but that doesn't stop him from thinking he's the toughest lion hunter around (especially in the wooded country we just moved to). He has Addison's disease, but thanks to everyone at Elkhart Veterinary Clinic we get to enjoy him several more years. Being our only son, we love him very much!

SMOKEY THE BANDIT IV
LANGHORNE, PENNSYLVANIA

Bandit, a five-year-old, brown-and-black German Shepherd, has a definite mind of his own. An excellent watchdog, he protects his home with such vengeance that he greets guests in the driveway and escorts them into the house. Bandit's favorite stuffed plaything, Bear, has endured stitches all over his body. His hobbies are riding in the family pickup with his master, chasing rabbits that are too fast, and getting groomed by the central vacuum. By far his favorite pastime is lying down in our boat and overseeing bass fishing for hours. Bandit, if you read this— your master loves you!

SMOKEY REYES
SHERMAN OAKS, CALIFORNIA

Smokey was found skinny, abandoned, hungry for food and love. All it took was one can of dog food and some water and he was ours forever. Smokey enjoys getting fat and barking at rocks until they go deaf. He also enjoys swimming in pools, lakes and the ocean. When we call him to go outside, he ignores us because he doesn't want to leave his favorite corner of the house with his five stuffed animals.

SOMBRERO DECK
MARATHON, FLORIDA

Sombrero is an adorable black-and-white Border Collie who was rescued at three months by his owner Wayne from a life of hanging out at dumpsters. Sombrero is now two and half and loves to work with Wayne, swimming, retrieving, carrying coconuts, and snuggling with anyone. Though very obedient, Sombrero was a real terror in the chewing department for about two years—he ate sofas, chairs, drapes, and shoes. Wayne was patient and ultimately rewarded with one of the best dogs in the world. Sombrero rode out Hurricane Andrew with his friends in Marathon, Florida, while Wayne worried with his parents in Virginia.

SONAR BARGER
MELBOURNE, FLORIDA

Sonar is a five-year-old Golden Retriever. He is reddish-colored and loves to swim, chase cats, and carry things for miles. He is a Hearing Dog Guide, sponsored by a pilot program for the Vero Beach Humane Society and trained and certified by Florida Hearing Dog Guides. Brevard County now carries his name as the Sonar District. He is the first and, to date, the only dog badged by NASA and Government Security to accompany his mistress to work at Kennedy Space Center should it become necessary. He is eighty-five pounds of personality.

SOPHIE DOLAS
BERKELEY, CALIFORNIA

S ophie Dolas, a small Standard Poodle, has worked in American Regional Theater since she was three months old. As a technical theater assistant who specializes in mood engineering, she has participated in thirty-four professional productions in the past seven years. Her duties range from silent support to the raising of company morale. She has also worked as a teaching assistant at U.C. Berkeley and has toured California and Nevada with five Shakespearean productions, serving as an advance motel scout and luggage guard. Trained at the Sirius Puppy Training School in Berkeley, Sophie received the Bone of the Week Award for twelve consecutive weeks.

SPARKY BALLARD
VERO BEACH, FLORIDA

Sparky the Beagle is a working dog. No, not chasing rabbits as you might expect. He's "Roving Reporter" for *DogGone,* the newsletter about fun places to go and cool stuff to do with your dog. Sparky's traveled the United States, from New York to the Grand Canyon, from Savannah to San Francisco. His impressions are translated by Mom, publisher of *DogGone.* Sparky helps sniff out pet-friendly beaches, parks, and attractions. He's even been to Dollywood theme park in Tennessee!

SPARKY GILMAN
TEHACHAPI, CALIFORNIA

Sparky is a five-year-old tricolor Beagle mix. We adopted him at eight weeks from the humane society in Homestead, Florida. Our lives have been full of joy and happiness ever since. Sparky is loyal, lovable, obedient, and protective. As a connoisseur of fine cuisine, food is his friend! Sparky loves adventure and travel. He swam with alligators in the Everglades; he was eye-to-eye with buffalo in South Dakota; and during his explorations here in California he has successfully dodged all but one rattlesnake. Sparky has also acquired a goodly amount of frequent-flyer miles.

438

SPARKY "THE BUG" APONTE
PHILADELPHIA, PENNSYLVANIA

Sparky is a 2½-year-old Shetland Sheepdog. He is called "The Bug" because he is a very friendly, hyperactive and energetic dog who always wants you to play with him. He will bark at you, bring his toys and hit your leg until he gets you to play. He enjoys playing with toys, fetching balls and catching frisbees. He prefers cold weather and especially likes to run in the snow and go cross-country skiing. He is a connoisseur of food—he loves to eat anything and anytime. He is a very cherished companion and friend.

SPECK LOUISE WALL
INDEPENDENCE, MISSOURI

Speck is a five-year-old mixed breed dog who is gray with large black spots. Rescued from the clutches of death, this Pound Hound is a chosen child. Selected as a small puppy because of her petite size and cheerful, loving disposition, she rapidly blossomed into a sixty-pound bundle of joy. She is very playful and loves children. Speck entertains everyone with her amazing catching ability with both frisbee and tennis ball. She has a friendly and outgoing personality and introduced herself to the entire neighborhood as soon as she was able to jump the backyard fence.

SPIKE HARDESTY
WILLSEYVILLE, NEW YORK

An eleven-year-old Doberman, Spike is truly a junkyard dog. He has spent his life guarding the local used auto parts establishment and has done a tremendous job of it. His size alone would frighten any trespasser, and his bark makes the hair on the back of people's necks stand on end. Underneath his impressive appearance, however, Spike is really a baby at heart. If he knows you and you're a good person, he likes you. And if you bring him a treat, he loves you forever. If given a choice between treats or working, Spike will sit on the fence, so to speak, by growling while eating.

S.S.
AURORA, COLORADO

S.S. A funny name, but for a Springer Spaniel it fit so well. Some say S.S. resembled a small dairy cow because he was a little overweight and liked to eat grass! S.S. loved rides in the car, sliding down the slide at the park, and trying desperately to climb trees. Sometimes he wasn't so easy to get along with, but that was part of his personality. S.S. lived eight great years with us. He passed away in March of 1989.

STRIPE WIDNER
ARLINGTON, VIRGINIA

Stripe (AKC Blue Moon's Con Artist) is a purebred Dalmatian with roots in Catalonia, Spain. She loves to chew on green things, snacking on lettuce and broccoli, and once ate $2,400 of her dad's traveler's checks. Matriculating in obedience training at Catholic University of America, at her professor's insistence she pursued graduate studies. Stripe's pastime is tennis. Her game is to bring, without being detected, a tennis ball from the patio into the house and deposit it at the feet of her mom or dad, who then yells, "No balls in the house!" This creates the excitement of Match Point at Wimbledon.

SUNSHINE ("SUNNY") BRAXTON
HAMPTON, VIRGINIA

Sunshine is a mixed Chihuahua/Dachshund. She was a stray wearing no tags when I found her four years ago. Sunshine has no use for toys anymore. She's twelve years old and spends her afternoons sunbathing in her bed or sleeping buried in mine. She flirts with boy dogs a good thirty seconds until they've bored her; then she saunters off, cutting her eyes at them. Sunshine's favorite exercise is begging for food. Deeply concentrating, her eyes bore holes into your plate in hopes that the food will fall through; if that doesn't work, she honks (not barks) like a donkey.

SUZY CARTER
SAN BERNARDINO, CALIFORNIA

Suzy is an eleven-pound Bichon Frise. She never has been particularly interested in responding to "Suzy." For a brief period of time she answered only to "Ken," and she now prefers "Suzanne." When I enrolled Suzy in Gentle Puppy Training, our first direction was to leave our puppies in the waiting room, proceed to the training room, and the puppies would follow. All followed but Suzy, who hid behind the door and was squished as the remaining participants entered. Fortunately, Suzy has aged gracefully. She loves walks, and the neighborhood children adore her. Suzy is a dear, funny little dog, the joy of my life.

SYDNEY VALKYRIE ORLEANS GRAHAM
BERKELEY, CALIFORNIA

Sydney was born in 1980 under the sign of Sagittarius. Her spiritual adviser has determined that she is in fact the reincarnation of Marie Curie, a genius trapped in a dog's body. The dog's body itself is so outstanding that Sydney is a virtual Helen of Troy among Dalmatians. She is a true Diana Artemis, able to hunt and run with the best of them. Her particular interest is haute cuisine, and she spends a great deal of time searching the garbage cans and alleys of Berkeley in an attempt to unearth epicurean delights. Sydney has an intensely affectionate nature.

T-BO MILLER
REDDING, CALIFORNIA

Born August 1, 1986, in Reno, Nevada, T-Bo has toured some of the West. Moving to Redding, California, for ten months after giving Reno two good years, he then gave Greater Los Angeles a try. Ninety days later he was back in Redding for a while. T-Bo, named after a famous character in the cartoon *The Ewoks,* doesn't resemble him at all. Being part Golden Retriever and Akita, he tips the scales at 118 pounds and is black with a white chest area. When not lounging, he rides in his Jeep Cherokee, which bears his name on the license plate.

TAIGO ROTSTEN
SYLMAR, CALIFORNIA

Taigo is a male Alaskan Malamute. Rescued as a stray, he now lives with three cats, an owner, and the owner's spouse. Taigo is black and white, weighs eighty pounds, and stands twenty-five inches at the withers. He is friendly and loved by all. Taigo rides to the office where his owner, Michael, practices Animal Rights law in Encino, California. Taigo has settled his own injury case by having his paw print notarized, now considered an act of notoriety among attorneys.

TALLY-HO
OSSINING, NEW YORK

Tally, age five, is a black-and-white Norwegian Elkhound. She spends her days protecting the yard, barking at everyone and everything—even a leaf blowing in the wind. Sometimes she just likes to relax in the shade. She also enjoys escaping through the fence. We should have called her Houdini. Tally's pastimes are being petted by anyone, eating, and shedding.

TAMMY VICTORIA SMITH
ROANOKE, VIRGINIA

I first saw Tammy in the back of a car driven by a lady searching the neighborhood for the abandoned dog's owner. Several days later the lady came back to me, explaining that she couldn't keep the dog. I gladly accepted since I'd thought of nothing but this cute little black-and-white puppy. Named in honor of Tammy Wynette, she was bred to a certain little black George Jones and I still have one of their puppies—a short, long-haired white Dolly (as in Parton). Tammy and Dolly are inseparable and have given me so much happiness.

TANYA ("BOO BOO") TAWNS
FT. LAUDERDALE, FLORIDA

Tanya is a big, black, friendly Doberman. She has beautiful markings and long legs that love to run. Occasionally she makes a break for freedom when we carelessly open the door. She throws back her ears and gallops around the neighborhood like a Greyhound. Soon the police cars are chasing her since people are afraid of her size, not knowing what a big baby she is. After dinner Tanya sits and stares at you, with the odd prod from her paw, until you produce the cookies and milk! Once that's done, it's off to bed.

451

TARA IRWIN
RICHLAND, WASHINGTON

Tara is a fourteen-year-old, seventeen-pound black-and-white Terrier mix. Her favorite activities have included: bobbing for ice cubes in the bathtub; taking running jumps on our bed (and sometimes missing!); trying to bury treats and chew toys in the carpet; and getting our boys in trouble by making "I'm in serious pain" yips while they're playing. (She has never understood our need for children when we already had her!) Tara is very annoyed by bows in her hair after grooming and by being left home alone. She is addicted to pretzels.

TARA "T" LAVINO
WAWARSING, NEW YORK

Born September 1991, Tara is a beautiful buckskin American Pit Bull Terrier. She is very affectionate and playful. On our arrival home we are usually greeted by Tara sitting on a table so she can see us through the window. Tara loves to be held and to go for walks. She lets us know when it is time to walk by sitting and staring at us until we get her leash. At night, of course, she sleeps on our bed. Tara has many admirers and she knows we all love her.

TARKA
DURHAM, NORTH CAROLINA

Tarka, born February 7, 1987, is a black Labrador with royal blood. He has the same bloodline as the Queen of England's Labs. Tarka emigrated in 1990 from England. His favorite game is climbing the fence out of the backyard and walking along the Eno River. He loves to chase rabbits and actually caught one once, but didn't know what to do with it. He brings a shoe when he wants to go out, his favorite chair is the one his owner has just gotten out of, and he swims in muddy pools, only using the swimming pool to drink from.

TASADAY
CHICAGO, ILLINOIS

Tassy, a Scottish Terrier waif, was found living on the streets. She was rescued and estimated to be about four years old. She took her mom to obedience school. There were thirty-five pupils, and Tasaday was valedictorian. Tassy and Mom feel that people considering a new addition to the family should go to their shelter. (Twenty-two million animals a year are put to death because there are no homes for them. Twenty-five percent of the animals in shelters are purebreds!) Tassy's favorite pastime is to dig and roll around in the bed, a practice referred to as "Rootin' and Tootin'."

TASHA ("TISSY POO") PAUL
LAKEWOOD, COLORADO

Tasha is an eight-year-old spayed silver Bouvier des Flandres who was abandoned when she was a year old and is especially bonded to me. She loves to watch things and is fascinated by TV, objects blowing on the ground, and even fish swimming in aquariums. She is affectionate but does not demand attention and is very contented when being petted. She loves to luxuriate in snow or mud puddles to cool off. Tasha is a Therapy Dog at a local hospital where the patients enjoy her very much. She enjoys the patients, too.

TASHA SLAUGHTER
NEWBURGH, NEW YORK

Tasha is a nine-year-old Lhasa Apso who has lived with us for five years now. Along with patrolling her home and yard, Tasha now has a job with me at the Hawaiian Harbor Tanning and Health Spa in Newburgh. After our morning walk to greet the other merchants, Tasha is very busy greeting our customers at the door (where they rub her tummy) and then escorting them through the store—it's a perfect job for Tasha since she likes to go everywhere with me and meet new people.

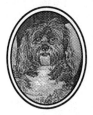

TAUSHA
BRIDGEPORT, CONNECTICUT

No one knows how old Tausha really is. She has outlived most trees. A true Siberian Husky, her sky-blue eyes and cloud-white face still make her look puppy-like. Tausha, having the patience of a mom, is working on her second generation of children. Between the tail-pulling, ear-poking, and hugging, she still maintains her composure. When other dogs come to visit, she is a great hostess and shows them all the fun spots in the yard. She will also sit down and tell them stories of the good old days. A snoozer beyond compare, she is what a friend should be.

TAWA KACHINA TAVA
KEY LARGO, FLORIDA

Tawa is a true laid-back Florida Keys "Conch" dog! He is an eighty-five-pound, white half Australian Sheepdog and half Labrador. Tawa was born with a very pale pink nose, which invited skin cancer, so his parents had his nose tattooed a solid black color. It looks extremely dapper and is a guarantee against the dangerous rays of the sun. Tawa is famous in the fabulous Florida Keys for his beautiful nose— and soul! His favorite games are tug-toy and minnow-stompin' on his beach. He is named for the sun spirit Kachina.

TAYLOR MARIE CULLEN
AKRON, OHIO

Taylor is a Beagle mix whose favorite phrase is "Have mercy on me!" She was abused as a puppy but now revels in adoration and comfort. Her favorite pastime is listening to classical music and watching the squirrels and birds from my window. She loves to sleep on the landing going upstairs at night "just in case" any weird sounds or noises are going on. She's very maternal and knows when anyone is in a depressed mood. She believes love alone can cure anything—and when she lays her head in your lap you can almost believe it.

TEDDI BELLE WILLIAMS
HUNTINGTON, WEST VIRGINIA

Teddi is a seven-month-old black Pomeranian puppy. She loves to play chase and tug-of-war with her toys. One of her favorite toys is a small brown fur-covered monkey. He is referred to as Teddi's boyfriend. If she brings her monkey to you and you ignore her, she will butt him against you until you play. Teddi also loves to hide her bones. Even if there is nothing to cover a bone with, she will *pretend* to hide it by scooting imaginary covers over it with her nose, thinking no one can see it. What a dog!

TEDDY "THE WOO"
RYE BROOK, NEW YORK

The Woo was a Collie. He loved Fridays, shopping day and toy day. He would go through all the bags for his new toy. His collection grew until he had his own toy box. He would open the lid with his nose and hold it open with his head. He would get you any toy you asked for. He learned tricks very fast. He climbed ladders, sat on stools, made noises like an airplane, rolled over and over, crawled on his belly like a soldier, and called me Mom on the phone. A real fun circus dog.

TEDDY McCORD
(MY PRECIOUS TEDD)
TUCSON, ARIZONA

T eddy is a very small Yorkshire Terrier who alternates between being an angel and a gremlin. He has a black-and-gray body, ginger-colored face, and big brown eyes. Teddy likes to play hide-and-seek. He thinks that if he hides just his head, no one can find him. To get your attention, he'll take his left paw and hit you across the leg. He also uses his paw to swat his sister Mindy across the face so she'll chase him.

TEDDY "TEDERICO," "TED BEAT" JOYNT
GALESVILLE, MARYLAND

Teddy, a Bichon Frise, was born in 1990 in Middleburg, Virginia. His friends are also Bichons—Wally and Betsy. A year later, his favorite human was born, Spencer. Teddy has city and country homes, but he prefers the country for the abundance of puddles, mud and goose droppings to be found there. A day is not complete without a good roll in the mud, followed by a roustabout with Betsy, Wally or Spencer and then a good night's sleep on Mom or Dad's head. He understands many words, but his favorites are "Bye-Bye," which means off-to-the-country, and "Milkbone."

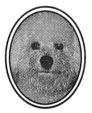

TEE-JONTUE ("HONEY BUN") ENTREKIN
OCEAN SPRINGS, MISSISSIPPI

Honey Bun is a three-pound apricot Toy Poodle. He is ten years old and would never believe he's a dog if someone were to tell him. He loves the car and rides on my left arm for hours on a trip. He sleeps on my legs at night and dares me to move; if I do, the groan starts and doesn't stop until I do. He can make his ears stand up and he has lost some of his front teeth, so when you say "Outside" (his favorite word) his ears go up, his tongue goes out to one side, and he looks like an Ewok!

TENNESSEE WHISKEY RIVER ("WHISKERS")
WHITE LAKE, WISCONSIN

Whiskey is the All-American dog (America, the melting pot of the world). His real daddy was a stranger in the night. He was adopted at our local shelter. Whiskey is black with dark coloring around his feet and chest. His favorite hobbies are chewing his dish and closing the trash can lids. He is the adopted son of our older dog (Brandy), who just loves him to pieces and has this in mind sometimes when he thinks his puppy is pestering him. Anyway, Whiskey is the best addition to our little family (even Brandy agrees). We love you, Whiskers.

TEX HALL
NEW YORK, NEW YORK

B orn of pedigree parentage on Long Island, Tex found himself unacceptable to folks at the WKC because of the dappled markings on his forehead and chest. Undaunted by this social slight, he moved to the heart of the Big Apple, New York City's Central Park South, also establishing strong social contacts in Dallas (Sophie, Golden Retriever) and Buffalo Gap (Gus, mutt), where he occasionally finds respite from his vocation as Ambassador of Good Will. Usually surrounded by tourists, he is equally at home amidst the horse-drawn carriages of the city and rounding up longhorn cattle in Texas.

TIMMY KIESZKA DEINZER
CHICAGO, ILLINOIS

Timmy is a fourteen-year-old Dachshund with brown and black markings. He is standard size, meaning he has the bark of a German Shepherd, which he uses against all he considers intruders, especially UPS men. His hobbies include hiding heartworm pills under the dishwasher and enjoying gourmet food—he loves toasted croutons. Sometimes, however, he succumbs to the temptation of junk foods, especially soup bones. When finished with them, he drops them in his master's cowboy boots. Although this is a completely self-taught trick, his creative genius is *not* appreciated!

TINY COKER
PICAYUNE, MISSISSIPPI

Not a classic name given by Connie Jo and Terry for our Class AAA Bull Terrier. From a tiny town in Texas, this tiny newborn became the family love and joy. She had hand-held ice-cream cones when the children had theirs. Upon moving to a new split-level house, she was told only once not to go up the one and a half steps to other parts of the house from her spacious den. She has never disobeyed! Once she won first prize for the dog with the shortest tail. Love for her is indescribable and infinite.

TIPHANY CLOVER, V.C.C.; TD, INC.
EAST LYME, CONNECTICUT

Six year old Clover (with her puppy-like antics) has brought nothing but love and joy to all who've met her since we rescued her at six months of age. She loves playing, but she equally loves therapy dog work where she gives kisses to anyone desiring them. Knee surgery left her with some limitations (like not being able to be a working sled dog), but she truly enjoys life. Although she experienced some type of prior abuse, she's turned out to be a very loving, trusting and giving dog. She will always be our "Perpetual Puppy!"

TODFIELD'S TRISTAN II
TRIBES HILL, NEW YORK

Tristan is a Red Grizzle Border Terrier born July 9, 1989. Originally a Hoosier, he joined his family in Georgia as a special surprise for his daddy's birthday. Since that time he has relocated with his family to Upstate New York, where he greatly prefers the climate. He dislikes hot weather, uncooked food, Schnauzers, and clear Gummy bears. He loves walks to the post office with Dad, sleeping in the middle of the bed, homemade dog biscuits, his toys "Little Blue" and "Little Red," riding in the car with the window down, and his "aunties," Border Collies Folly and Scone.

TONEE GIRL AHL
CHARLESTOWN, MARYLAND

Tonee is a nine-year-old, 103-pound Siberian Husky. Her beautiful face is always the first thing that people comment on. Tonee is very gentle and loves kittens. She has, on many occasions, chased the neighbor's cat away from her kittens in order to carry them individually to her own home to clean them and pretend to nurse them. She does not share her brother Hutch's enthusiasm for retrieving. In fact, she often wears a pink bandanna that reads "Ah, Go Fetch It Yourself." Tonee does like car rides and especially her treats.

TOOTS' PRINCESS MATILDA ("TILLIE")
BARBOURSVILLE, WEST VIRGINIA

Tillie is a black Labrador Retriever who loves everyone. She enjoys walking in the woods, riding in the auto, and swinging in the porch swing before going to bed. She helps harvest everything from strawberries to potatoes (her big paws make them fly). She likes to carry the bucket or basket when we start to the garden. She carries sticks to the trash. I hold her collar while she helps me climb the hill. She is three years old now, and we find it necessary to spell certain words in her presence. A happy hundred pounds of love and fun!

TRIXIE (THE TRICKSTER) PANICO
SOMERS POINT, NEW JERSEY

T he newlyweds, Anthony and Mary Ann, made the mistake of visiting the local Humane Society Shelter and there she was—the world's cutest puppy! They left the shelter empty handed, but a mysterious force made them return to adopt that special little puppy. Now, only a year later, Trixie rules the roost! She is smart, cute, quick, and very cunning. In fact, there is some speculation that Trixie is actually a Wily Coyote in disguise because she certainly knows how to get what she wants. But in return: she speaks on command, fetches her ball, plays dead, and shakes hands.

TROTSKY WEISS
EAST GREENWICH, RHODE ISLAND

Trotsky (L.T. Weiss) is a full-blooded Shusky. He is five years old and has been graduated with honors from Stony Lane Kennels Obedience School. Trotsky is 100 pounds in weight and an excellent watchdog. He is particularly fond of every known food group. Of special note is his mention in the acknowledgments of two books, *Making It Work* and *Million Dollar Consulting,* under his formal name, L.T. Weiss, citing him for his "unerring editorial assistance."

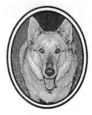

TUFFY ADOLPHSON
AURORA, ILLINOIS

Tuffy (nicknamed Tufer) is a fourteen-year-old white Miniature Poodle who loves attention and has never met anyone he does not like. When riding in a car, he insists on being in the front passenger seat even if it means the discomfort of sitting on someone's lap for hours. He is gentle and affectionate and likes to be with people. Tuffy is extremely alert to changes in his physical surroundings and will bark to let you know that a piece of furniture has been moved from its usual location or that a neighbor's children have new toys or play equipment in their yard.

TUKIE WEISS-ROGERS
(A.K.A. TUKAMO, TUKE)
MARIONVILLE, MISSOURI

I found Tukie, an abandoned puppy, in a New York City lot on the Fourth of July. With a slice of bologna we made friends, but his sad eyes begged for more. Impulsively I snuck him on the subway, where he readily slept, curled in my lap. That night his face wore such an expression of relief I had to keep him somehow. I called him "Tukie" for "to keep." However, months of altercations with my peevish cats demanded a compromise. So we drove a thousand miles to my sister's country acres, where he now lives with four dogmates, enjoying happiness, sunshine, and love.

TYLER MACDONALD IV
CHARLOTTETOWN, PRINCE EDWARD ISLAND, CANADA

I an and Olga have a six-year-old Doberman/ Shepherd/Pit Bull named Tyler. Several trees have been uprooted in the backyard, and three bathrooom doors have been replaced. Tyler sleeps on the bed; Ian and Olga sleep on the floor. Although Tyler is perceived to be friendly, the mail must now be picked up at the Postal Office. When Tyler brings home a bone, Ian takes it to the pathologist to assure it is of animal origin. Both Ian and the dog attended U.P.E.I.—the dog graduated.

TYNDARI VON ROSENBERG
BAYTOWN, TEXAS

D ari was a red Dachshund with black-outlined brown eyes in a beautiful, sensitive face. With a big bark that belied his size, he kept all "varmints" out of our territory. He loved to play with a slinky toy by holding the string in his teeth, walking backwards, and growling. He attacked hand-held puppets but disdained any "fetching" games. When five years old, he overcame a back operation to again become a happy forest trail companion. A diabetic, he accepted his shots without complaint and survived to bring us love and joy from November 21, 1972, to June 3, 1989.

UKE MCCONNELL
OCEANSIDE, CALIFORNIA

Uke is a Keeshond/Wolf mix. He is about ten years old, and I got him from a friend about six months ago. He is very playful and intelligent, a great guard dog and very protective. Uke loves his toys, old shoes, and bones. Sometimes he howls at night in a deep voice at the coyotes in the hills near our home. He's black, gray, and white, and very furry! He loves brushing and pats—the best dog I've ever had!

URI RESNICK
MIAMI BEACH, FLORIDA

U ri was a Bouvier des Flandres. He was big and (almost) black and beautiful. Uri was unbelievably cute, despite his size, and lots of fun. He would body-block you when playing in the yard, like the cattle herder he was bred to be, and lie in the doorway of whatever room you were in and chase around madly when you came home. He was absolutely gorgeous with this full, long shaggy, silky charcoal coat and wonderfully cuddly, and we loved him very, very much.

VALLEY BROOK'S NITID KISMET ("KIZZY") STAPLES
LOUISVILLE, TENNESSEE

Kismet is a beautiful sable German Shepherd from the same bloodlines as the famous New Skete dogs. Now five years old, she spent most of her life in south Florida. She is certified through Therapy Dogs, Inc., and spent almost two years doing pet therapy at New Medico of Palm Beach, Florida. She obeys verbal commands, hand signals, and also A.S.L.! Most famous for her "play dead" and "roll over," she is also obsessed with tennis balls and her four Siamese cats. Despite her seventy-pound size, Kis is always extremely gentle with babies, children, handicapped people, and the elderly.

VALLEY GIRL COTTON
AUSTIN, TEXAS

Valley Girl was found by her humans October 30, 1986, eating food in the middle of the intersection at R.R. 620 and Great Valley Drive. She was about eight months old and part Border Collie. Valley is a very loving dog. When you ask her "Do you love me, Valley?" she will put her front leg around you and give you a hug. She was the wife of Bronson and good mother to seven pups. Valley loves playing fetch with a ball or a frisbee. And she loves herding the Cottons' cats in the true Border Collie style.

VARGO VOM CASTELL-BERNAUER
LAWTON, OKLAHOMA

V argo Vom Castell-Bernauer, better known as Dagger, was born May 11, 1987, in Frankfurt, Germany. He is a typical red longhaired Dachshund, uppity and independent. He came to the United States in December of 1987. His favorite pastime is digging. He doesn't try to dig out of anywhere—he just digs deep, clean holes for everyone's enjoyment. His sister, Duchess, is his best friend, and he watches over her carefully. Dagger also believes he is part grasshopper. He will jump up on anything, no matter how high. Then he will ask for help to get down.

VELVET BOETTCHER
PORTLAND, OREGON

Velvet, a three-year-old black Lab/Shepherd/Border Collie mix, is a service dog. She assists me by retrieving dropped objects, carrying things in her backpack, and pulling my wheelchair when I get stuck, and she has brought me the telephone when I have fallen in the yard so I can call for help. Without Velvet I would require twenty-four-hour attendant care. My doctor now allows me to stay home alone after witnessing these services. Velvet does get time off to play tennis—she's quite good and very fast.

VICTORIA KEILHOFER QUINN
MARTINSBURG, WEST VIRGINIA

Victoria is a loyal and loving four-year-old black Labrador/Australian Shepherd pound puppy. She is very intelligent. From the very first day that I brought her home, and before retiring each evening, I will give her five kisses; if I inadvertently forget to give her the exact count, she will stick her head under my chin and push me until I respond. She loves to ride in the car and visit her cousin Crystal (a Pekingese). Her favorite activities are wrestling with the family, swimming, watching television, and waiting for commercials, because she knows food is involved

Waldo ("Wally") VanAlstyne
Denton, Texas

A 120-pound Lab, Wally (1972—1985) was beloved companion and gregarious namesake of Waldo's Bar (where he was in charge of greeting, sniffing, scarfing burgers, and sleeping on the couch). Once lost for three days he found his way home by identifying a neighbor's car, waiting by it, and barking incessantly when the driver returned. Would, upon command, go upstairs and wait in the dreaded bathtub. Would also get in the designated seat and vehicle of his owners, unless he was going to the Vet—then he would get into anybody else's. Spoiled and overfed, he was a happy dog. We miss him.

WALDO MAXXIMILLION NAYLOR
BLOOMINGTON, CALIFORNIA

W aldo is a seventy-five-pound Old English Sheepdog, born March 17, 1992. He is a large, lovable dog. After having hip displasia and surgery before the age of one year, he has turned out to be very strong but also a big baby. Waldo likes to pick up his food dish and take it to his blanket so he can lie down and eat. He would probably do that with the water bucket, too, if he could lift it. He also likes to chew on everything in sight and then, when he gets caught, look at me like, "What did I do?"

WARLOCK'S LITTLE DREAM WEAVER, CDX ("MICHA")
NIKISKI, ALASKA

Micha, age eleven and a half, is a Schipperke with two AKC obedience titles, trophies, and ribbons. She lives for food and belly rubs. But last year, when the spring thaws came and there was flooding because the sewer pipes were still frozen and not draining, Micha saved the day. The Alaska State Department of Transportation could not figure out how to get thaw wire through the existing pipe, and Micha was called upon to pull cord through 1,750 feet of eighteen-inch pipe! She received statewide front-page coverage and a letter from the Governor! She's wonderful.

WEBSTER ("PUPLET") BAUER
NORWALK, CONNECTICUT

Webster is a small, long, adorable dog. He is half Dachshund, half Terrier. He loves to look out any and all windows. He sleeps in bed with his parents, under the covers in winter. He barks at squirrels and cats, and he enjoys taking walks with his dad. He also expects a Milkbone every time he comes back from a walk. Webster and his mother placed first in a pet-owner look-alike contest, and his mother couldn't be more pleased! Webster's favorite activities include: chasing balls, running around with socks, and, most importantly, licking everybody he can.

WEDGEWOOD WHITWORTH
LAREDO, TEXAS

W edge, a King Charles Spaniel, was born August 19, 1992, in Madison, Virginia. At the tender age of ten weeks he flew by himself to his new home in Laredo, Texas, and to his new family, Steve, Alice, Annie, and Lizzie. Wedge is intelligent, all dog (though small—twelve pounds), and very civilized. His friendly personality endears him to everyone and he pretty much gets his way. His favorite pastimes are playing (abusing) his collection of stuffed animals, retrieving his ball, and riding in the car—especially to the ranch, where he barks at the cattle from a safe distance. We love you, Wedge!

WHITNEY
BUELLTON, CALIFORNIA

Whitney is a sweet and sensitive American Eskimo dog, five years old, who loves to bark and play and has no idea what being a real dog is all about. Although she is very affectionate and loves to cuddle, she insists on sleeping by herself in my car at night. We think she craves the solitude and quiet. We bought Whitney on an impulse when she was six weeks old (there is nothing cuter than an American Eskimo puppy) and used to call her "Monster Puppy" because she was so incredibly energetic. We wouldn't take a million dollars for her—or ever get another American Eskimo!

WHO-TWO MCELVEEN
VERSAILLES, KENTUCKY

Who-Two was a Rhodesian Ridgeback who lived to be ten years old. She was bred to hunt lions, and all the years she lived with us in Idaho and Kentucky we never once saw a lion—so she certainly did her job well!

WHOOPI MONTGOMERY
CHARLESTON, WEST VIRGINIA

Her name is Whoopi, but her face is unknown. She is a black Shih Tzu whose facial hair hides what must be an interesting set of expressions. She's very courageous for such a small dog, but her size has allowed her to escape the backyard fence and lead her brother on a real world excursion. Whoopi is afraid of heights, loud noises, and cars, but brave enough to eat houseplants and bark at neighbor dogs through the window. She and her brother appreciate their size. They get carried almost everywhere they go!

WHOOZIT
BUELLTON, CALIFORNIA

Whoozit (Who is it?) is a small black puréed breed dog—even the vet can't quite figure out his lineage. He was seen one morning on the freeway, filthy and frozen with fear. He quickly endeared himself to his rescuer, and when no one claimed him it soon became apparent he had found a home. Whoozit has many behavior problems stemming from apparent abuse and neglect, but with love and patience he has blossomed into a secure and wonderful dog. His favorite pastime is hanging out the window on car trips, his ears flapping in the breeze as he sniffs new and wonderful smells.

WINDAMOHRS MAXWELL WILLIAMS
DURHAM, NORTH CAROLINA

Max the Basset was born February 12, 1986, and comes from a long bloodline of champions. He's very stubborn and always gets his own way. Being the ruler of his house and yard, he loves to chase the birds and squirrels away from their feeders to show them who is in command. Besides sleeping and eating, he has his favorite toys, Mr. Orange (with sunglasses) and Mr. Porcupine. He loves the word "go" but not when it means to the vet's, where Dr. Reynolds hopes the moaning and growling just from cutting his toenails doesn't scare his other patients away.

WOLF STACEY
BIRMINGHAM, ALABAMA

A family member for seventeen years, Wolf provided comedy, love, laughter, joy, patience, and tears. He had a joyful bark, a pixie expression, and a bouncy walk. Wolf appreciated the smallest favors, treats, and rewards. He made vacations exciting and rewarding. On lonely beaches he explored every hole, mound, and piece of debris, a free spirit. When Wolf sat up and extended his paws, a heart of stone was turned to jelly. The Stacey family was indeed fortunate in having Wolf Stacey share his life with us.

YOSEMITE
GLENDALE, CALIFORNIA

Her mother and eight one-day-old puppies were abandoned at the pound. Yosemite was the friendliest and funniest of the litter and eight months later has become an enthusiastic swimmer, ball-catcher, and stick-fetcher. If I let her, she sleeps with her head on the pillows of my bed, and she walks around on her hind legs if she thinks it will get her treats. As eager as she is to learn whatever I teach her, I have to conclude that she is the Best Pet. Period.

YOU 'R' MY SUNSHINE (ROCKY ARRUZZA)
LANCASTER, SOUTH CAROLINA

Rocky is a five-year-old Great Dane. He is a brindle, which consists of gold and black stripes with a white bow-tie patch on his chest. He thinks he is small and tries to act little, although in reality he is close to 200 pounds and stands just over 36 inches tall! He loves to play with his toys, especially a huge sneaker and a large rawhide bone. Whenever he hears the refrigerator door open, he's there waiting with his eighteen-inch tail hitting whatever is handy. Needless to say, our house is not ever in danger of being burglarized.

YURY (SOCCER-DOG) HOPKINS
SPOKANE, WASHINGTON

Yury, handsome and dashing pet of Mr. and Mrs. John Hopkins, is an energetic three-year-old male dog of mixed breed. He has beautiful dark brown eyes, a medium-length coat (brown, black, and white), ears with a personality of their own, a long body and short legs, and a curving white-tipped tail that he waves as a flag of friendship. He resembles a cross between a Beagle, a Terrier, and a Dachshund. He loves chasing a basketball, playing tug-of-war, snacking on cheese, watching for cats, and napping on his fake fur bed in the afternoon.

ZAK FOUT
YELLOW SPRINGS, OHIO

*Z*ak is a ten-year-old tan English-Irish Setter with a white chest, a white-tipped tail, and a white stripe on his forehead. His favorite activities include running, chasing squirrels, playing ball, riding in cars, walks in the woods, and visiting his cousins Beau and Muff. Zak is very mellow, although he does enjoy attacking your feet when you walk near his biscuits. If nobody walks by, he will place a biscuit by your foot and then attack it! But any dog who loves soy cheese pizza and has a great smile always has a place called home.

ZEPPO OSBORN
(A.K.A. THE BIG GUY)
BROOMFIELD, COLORADO

Z eppo Osborn is a seven-year-old, seventy-five-pound rescued brindle Greyhound who, having retired from the fast life, has settled in to being the best friend his owner Jeff has ever had. Jeff's wife, Maryse, is certain that Zeppo is Jeff in dog form. The Big Guy's favorite words, "road trip," "walkies," and "treaties," cause him to lose all of his normal laid-back composure. Since December of 1992, Zeppo has been a Prescription Pet at The Children's Hospital, where he brings a little cheer to sick kids who can't see their own dogs and his big heart is opened to share.

ZUMA JAY RISENHOOVER
NASHVILLE, TENNESSEE

orn July 28, 1992, Zuma is a large, lovable white dog. He is a typical Great Pyrenees and loves lots of attention. He can lie with me on the coach for hours, never needing to move. When he gets out of his lazy mood, he likes to go play with his girlfriend, Dakota Marie Risenhoover. Lazy Zuma has gotten a bit chubby at 105 pounds, and has a tendency to jump on top of Dakota to win his favorite toy. They have great fun together, and we all love each other very much.